THE U⌐ D1648451

Does the unconscious exist and if so what does it do to us?
Antony Easthope looks for answers not deep inside but in
what people say and do every day without considering it.
Lucid, accessible and often funny, the book shows the reality
of the unconscious with a stunning variety of examples: from
jokes and rugby songs to *Hamlet*, Hitchcock's *Psycho* and the
life and death of Princess Di.

The idea of the unconscious changes the way we think about
identity, sexuality, history, art and literature. The conclusion
draws on psychoanalysis to discuss Stalin's Russia, Nazism
and the 'Final Solution'.

Antony Easthope is Professor of English and Cultural Studies
at Manchester Metropolitan University and author of
Englishness and National Culture (Routledge 1999).

THE NEW CRITICAL IDIOM

SERIES EDITOR: JOHN DRAKAKIS, UNIVERSITY OF STIRLING

The New Critical Idiom is an invaluable series of introductory guides to today's critical terminology. Each book:

- provides a handy, explanatory guide to the use (and abuse) of the term
- offers an original and distinctive overview by a leading literary and cultural critic
- relates the term to the larger field of cultural representation.

With a strong emphasis on clarity, lively debate and the widest possible breadth of examples, *The New Critical Idiom* is an indispensable approach to key topics in literary studies.

- Other books in the series.

Colonialism/Post colonialism by Ania Loomba
Gothic by Fred Botting
Historicism by Paul Hamilton
Humanism by Tony Davies
Ideology by David Hawkes
Literature by Peter Widdowson
Metre, Rhythm and Verse by Philip Hobsbaum
Myth by Laurence Coupe
Pastoral by Terry Gifford
Romanticism by Aidan Day
Sexuality by Joseph Bristow
Stylistics by Richard Bradford

THE UNCONSCIOUS

Antony Easthope

LONDON AND NEW YORK

First published 1999
by Routledge
11 New Fetter Lane, London EC4P 4EE

Simultaneously published in the USA and Canada
by Routledge
29 West 35th Street, New York, NY 10001

Routledge is an imprint of the Taylor & Francis Group

© 1999 Antony Easthope

The right of Antony Easthope to be identified as the Author
of this Work has been asserted by him in accordance with
the Copyright, Designs and Patents Act 1988

Typeset in Adobe Garamond and Scala Sans by Keystroke,
Jacaranda Lodge, Wolverhampton
Printed and bound in Great Britain by Clays Ltd, St Ives plc

British Library Cataloguing in Publication Data
A catalogue record for this book is available from the British Library.

Library of Congress Cataloguing in Publication Data
A catalogue record for this book has been requested.

ISBN 0–415–19208–0 (hbk)
ISBN 0–415–19209–9 (pbk)

For Diane

CONTENTS

SERIES EDITOR'S PREFACE

The New Critical Idiom is a series of introductory books which seeks to extend the lexicon of literary terms, in order to address the radical changes which have taken place in the study of literature during the last decades of the twentieth century. The aim is to provide clear, well-illustrated accounts of the full range of terminology currently in use, and to evolve histories of its changing usage.

The current state of the discipline of literary studies is one where there is considerable debate concerning basic questions of terminology. This involves, among other things, the boundaries which distinguish the literary from the non-literary; the position of literature within the larger sphere of culture; the relationship between literatures of different cultures; and questions concerning the relation of literary to other cultural forms within the context of interdisciplinary studies.

It is clear that the field of literary criticism and theory is a dynamic and heterogeneous one. The present need is for individual volumes on terms which combine clarity of exposition with an adventurousness of perspective and a breadth of application. Each volume will contain as part of its apparatus some indication of the direction in which the definition of particular terms is likely to move, as well as expanding the disciplinary boundaries within which some of these terms have been traditionally contained. This will involve some re-situation of terms within the larger field of cultural representation, and will introduce examples from the area of film and the modern media in addition to examples from a variety of literary texts.

Preface

Thirty years ago most people with liberal and progressive views believed that a large part of human unhappiness was caused by economic and social conditions. Get rid of poverty and injustice – people would be happy. Since then the majority of people throughout the Western world have acquired prosperity and social opportunities they never dreamed of before. Even so, many old forms of unhappiness remain and new ones have developed. Statistics for depression, suicide, alcohol and drug abuse are all a lot higher in Britain now than they were in 1955.

Why does someone keep having the same disastrous relationship with different partners? Why does another repeatedly enter into love affairs enthusiastically only to run from them the moment they look like taking off? Why do so many couples begin passionately in love only to find seven years and two children later that their partner is insufferably boring or irritating or worse? Why does an able, affectionate and intelligent boy from a loving family reach the age of thirteen, get in with the 'wrong crowd' at school and move from truancy to petty crime to hard drugs, breaking his mother's heart along the way?

Forty per cent of children in England go to sleep each night in a home with only one of their natural parents. Poverty still puts a strain on marriages, but it's not the only reason parents leave each other. Someone stuck in a violent or bitterly loveless relationship has to get out. But children would almost always prefer parents to stay together if they could. When he was twelve my son had a friend at school; in the afternoon he could go to his mother's, his father's, or his granny's, but the truth was that none of them wanted him.

I didn't really fancy reading Gordon Burns' book *Happy Like Murderers* about Fred and Rosemary West, both sexually abused as children, who went on to torture and dismember twelve young women, including some of their *own children*. In a review Melanie Phillips said the couple 'were not evil in the metaphysical sense'. Rather they were the products of a culture 'of fractured identities, violence, cruelty, transient relationships and, above all, neglected, abused and unloved children' (*TLS*, 9 October 1998). As I read it the theory of the unconscious has a clear message: try to look after the kids.

We need the concept of the unconscious today because it addresses questions of human happiness and unhappiness which come up *beyond* economic and social causes and conditions. Psychoanalysis has its problems but (except for religion) there's not much else on offer.

Born in 1958, Diana Spencer died in Salpêtrière hospital in Paris in 1997. She never experienced economic deprivation. When she was six her mother left home. At nineteen Diana lived out what may be a fantasy for many little girls by marrying a prince, though soon found he had taken up again with a long-time lover. She got ill. On 20 November 1995, in a television interview, she had this to say:

> I have had bulimia for a number of years. And that's like a secret disease. You inflict it upon yourself because your self-esteem is at a low ebb, and you don't think you're worthy or valuable. You fill your stomach up . . . and it gives you a feeling of comfort. It's like having a pair of arms round you. . . . It was a symptom of what was going on in my marriage. I was crying out for help but giving the wrong signals . . .
>
> (*Guardian*, 21 November 1995)

Diana understood her bulimia as a psychosomatic symptom, a displaced and *unconscious* expression of her insecurity and desire for love. The British monarchy is a social fraction not noted for the rapidity of its intelligence or openness to avant-garde ideas. When a member of this group shows an awareness of the basic notion of the unconscious, it's a sign that it has reached almost every level of modern society.

My account of the unconscious will aim to be clear, accessible and uncomplicated. In a short book I cannot claim to present a comprehensive analysis – my discussion will be confined to those writers who attract interest today, Freud and the French psycho-analyst who followed him, Jacques Lacan. Even with this limitation I shall have to omit quite a lot (readers will have to go elsewhere for discussion of the case histories or psychopathology).

I will not be able to describe adequately how individual writers changed their views. Lacan, for instance, seems to have found it difficult to maintain a consistent position across one lecture, let alone each year's syllabus of twenty. The material is uneven – some is easy to agree with, while other parts make most people sceptical.

My discussion of the unconscious is inflected towards areas of special interest to those concerned with literature, media and culture generally; hence chapters on 'The unconscious and the text' and 'The unconscious and history'. On some topics it is not hard to achieve objectivity: the unconscious is not one of these. Even if I tried I could not hide an enthusiasm for psychoanalysis and its insights into what people may be like. I would guess this is partly driven by a feeling that if I've had to put up with the unconscious all my life then no-one should be allowed to think they're free from it. No text is immune from desire, not even this one (reading it over I have a suspicion it contains an above-average number of dead or missing fathers).

I am very grateful to Jody Ball for finding a number of mistakes I had missed, especially a line from a song I really should have known. I would like to thank John Drakakis for an informed, conscientious, line-by-line correction of the manuscript, one which did not miss the sentence in which I referred to 'the treat of castration' rather than 'the threat of castration'. And finally Ian Parker for a number of acute comments, in particular for pointing out a serious aspect of Freud's theory in which I imagined he had said what I wanted him to say.

I have marked '*sic*' only for the first instance when a cited text uses a masculine term to mean men and women.

1

IS THERE AN UNCONSCIOUS?

'WOMAN FAINTS EVERY TIME SHE HEARS THE WORD SEX.'
(Headline in *Daily Mirror*, 15 July 1993)

This was the story of a woman who did indeed faint when she heard the word 'sex' and of a man who, having found out about what the paper called 'her bizarre condition', exploited it to molest her while she was unconscious. The case came to court but with the difficulty that every time the defence lawyer used the word 'sex' the woman fainted again. When another word was used – 'nookie' – the woman did not faint.

I mention this sad and grotesque story because it seems such a clear instance of an unconscious effect. What caused this dramatic physical effect was not an event or an action but a *meaning*, though admittedly a highly charged one. And it's not strictly a meaning which produced the fainting (the synonym 'nookie' didn't do it) but a specific set of sounds, a single signifier: 'sex'.

If there is an unconscious process it will be at work all the time, not just in spectacular one-off occasions like this. It will be a kind of lining on the other side of normal, waking consciousness which might not be noticed unless there was an effect over and above anything rational consciousness might expect and can explain. So it is with the following newspaper story about people campaigning against the use of animal fur. Now there is a reasonable case both for and against the use of fur: what is significant is the degree of *affect*, an intensity of feeling which far exceeds anything one might ordinarily predict.

Under the headline 'Keeping their fur on' (matched with a photograph of a beautiful woman with dark glasses wrapped in voluptuous furs), the *Independent on Sunday* reported a furrier, Lothar Weiss, explaining how business was going:

> Really terrible. My warehouse in Manchester has been attacked twice by the animal rights people – once with smoke bombs, and then with real bombs . . . it's made everyone afraid to sell or buy fur.
>
> (14 April 1991)

The story notes that in the seventies fur was not really an issue in Britain. However, 'a couple of decades on, thanks to Lynx and other anti-fur campaigners, it has become an act of daring to sport a splodge of beaver on your winter hat'.

Another furrier, Henri Kleiman, says about the anti-fur campaign:

> These people say revolting things. They imply furs are only worn by Knightsbridge bimbos who get them in return for sexual favours.

Surely there's an element of excess here – of aggression and excitement – which needs explaining? I would speculate as follows.

For the unconscious, animal fur, especially if long and elegant, only too easily symbolises pubic hair and particularly women's pubic hair. Imagined in this way a woman in a fur coat seems to be publicly flaunting her sexuality and transgressing Western codes about appropriate behaviour.

Two details in the story support this reading. The reference to wearing a 'splodge of beaver' echoes a slang word for women's pubic hair. And the idea that women who wear fur have acquired them via prostitution recalls the vulgar judgement (better known perhaps in the north of England) in which a flashy woman is said to be, 'all fur coat and no knickers'.

It is difficult to be sure what other explanations there could be for the surplus which oozes out of this story of the anti-fur campaigners. You could simply deny there *was* anything to be explained. But if an explanation is needed the idea of the unconscious can supply one. My version is consistent with details in the body of psychoanalytic writing – 'fur stands for the pubic hair', wrote Freud (1973–86, vol 4: 157) years before the anti-fur campaigners came on the scene with their bombs (both smoke and real, as Mr Weiss says). And Freud invoked the vulgar language of 'the people' to confirm psychoanalytic insights (I've drawn attention to 'beaver' and the phrase 'all fur coat and no knickers').

Freud suggests that we use symbolism with unconscious meaning all the time but conspire to ignore what we're doing. He supposes someone asking him the exasperated question, 'Do I really live in the thick of sexual symbols?' and if so how would you know? 'My reply', Freud says, 'is that we learn it from very different sources – from fairytales and myths, from buffoonery and jokes, from folklore (that is, from knowledge about popular manners and customs, sayings and songs) and from poetic and colloquial linguistic usage' (1973–86; vol 1: 192).

The question Freud asks himself, and his answer, points to a general principle. The concept of the unconscious bears with it the implication that people will often deny its existence so as to hold onto the (apparently) sane and ordinary world of everyday common sense.

So it should not come as a surprise if someone claimed there was no sexual connotation about 'beaver' *and* at the same time laughed at a joke which played on that double meaning (in the film parodying *Basic Instinct* the Sharon Stone figure parts her legs for the detectives – and reveals a large and attractively brown-eyed beaver perched there). It's significant that the word 'unconscious', meaning opposite to consciousness, is not in general currency but 'subconscious' is. 'Subconscious' carries the reassuring suggestion that the unconscious is only *sub*merged like a *sub*marine and can be brought to the surface when you want. Freud had explicitly given up 'subconscious' by 1900.

In fact, the unconscious – if it exists – is not a physical object you can put into a tube and test with chemicals. Its nature is inferred from an analysis of features in human behaviour – and particularly linguistic behaviour – which cannot be understood except on the hypothesis that there is an unconscious. The process is only apparent to us *indirectly*.

INNER SPEECH AND THE UNCONSCIOUS

A Russian linguist, L.S. Vygotsky, proposed a distinction between outer speech and inner speech – between articulated, external discourse and that 'voice' which goes on inside my head when I'm not talking to anyone. Vygotsky doesn't believe that inner speech is simply external speech which has been internalised – rather, inner speech has 'its own laws' (1962: 131). Generalising from the egocentric speech observed in children, Vygotsky supposed that inner speech had a certain specific style (peculiar syntax, repeated terms, discontinuity, etc.). Perhaps. But surely we can't fail to spot a serious epistemological problem hanging over his whole enterprise? We can only know about the inner speech of others from what they tell us, in outer speech. And that's not inner speech at all.

The question of unconscious thought has the same problematic status as inner speech – but with an added twist. In one respect it is harder to know about the unconscious than inner speech precisely because it is consciously repressed, actively unconscious (German: *unbewusst*). But for the same reason it's not harder to know about, because it is subject to the principle of psychoanalysis that 'the repressed returns'. Unlike inner speech, the unconscious 'speaks', willy-nilly, in all kinds of symptoms, traces, gaps, discontinuities and excesses that appear in ordinary conscious discourse. That phrase, 'splodge of beaver', articulates a repressed relationship between animal fur and female pubic hair, although the writer may not have been conscious of this relationship.

INSTINCT AND DRIVE

Today we have an exaggerated respect for the supposedly self-conscious rational individual, an idea we preserve by treating anything that is not part of consciousness as physical, an effect of the body. In Freud's carefully articulated explanation the unconscious is not part of the body but has a close relationship to it.

Freud was hugely influenced by Darwin's theory of evolution with its materialist and secular explanation of how life developed (see Sulloway 1980). Darwin argued that in order to succeed a species must develop not only instincts for survival (the theme of *The Origin of Species*, 1859) but also instincts for reproduction (which he wrote up in *The Descent of Man and Selection in Relation to Sex*, 1871). Freud suggested that the human species experiences not just instinct but *drive*, particularly in two forms – narcissism corresponding to the instinct for survival, and sexual desire corresponding to reproduction.

Drive (German: *Trieb*) is related to but profoundly different from instinct (German: *Instinkt*). Drive is instinct insofar as it has become represented. Freud says:

> an 'instinct' [*Trieb*] appears to us as a concept on the frontier between the mental and the somatic, as the psychical representative [*Repräsentant*] of the stimuli originating from within the organism and reaching the mind, as a measure of the demand made upon the mind for work in consequence of its connection with the body.
>
> ('Instincts and their Vicissitudes', 1973–86, vol 11: 118)

So, the human infant shares with other mammals an instinct which compels it to seek nourishment at the nipple. This instinct is very strong and very direct. Drive originates when there is a degree of separation between body and mind. An idea of or image of the nipple (along with associations of fulfilment) becomes remembered, a signifier which can become pleasurable in its own right – the symbol of the breast.

The situation is complicated by the fact that the standard English translation of Freud, trying to make psychoanalysis look more scientific, consistently translates *Trieb* as 'instinct'. The distinction should be quite clear, for as Freud explains:

> An instinct [*Trieb*] can never become an object of consciousness – only the idea [*Vorstellung*] that represents the instinct can. Even in the unconscious, moreover, an instinct cannot be represented otherwise than by an idea. If the instinct did not attach itself to an idea or manifest itself as an affective state, we would know nothing about it.
>
> (1973–86, vol 11: 179)

His point is that we don't 'know' about our irises contracting in bright light but we do 'know' about the image of the breast, for example. In psychoanalysis there is a continuing controversy about how far the body determines the forms of drive it initiates as well as the question of how far Freud is using the body as a metaphor for psychical processes. I shall stress that the unconscious is concerned above all with *meanings*, with symbols, a view which is quite unmistakable when Freud refers to 'the mother's penis' (1973–86, vol 7: 352), something unknown to physiology though it may be an object of fantasy for the unconscious.

The main evidence for the necessity of the concept of the unconscious occurs in certain specific forms of human behaviour, particularly:

- hypnosis;
- dreams;
- jokes;
- slips and everyday life;
- art;
- psychoanalytic case histories.

I shall say something about each of these, in part because set out in order like that they rather neatly recapitulate the development of Freud's ideas from around 1890 to 1910. At this stage I think we can go along with just the hypothesis that the unconscious seeks pleasure wherever it can, without being at all fussy about how it gets it, though it has the problem of finding a way round the surveillance of the conscious mind.

HYPNOSIS

Poets and artists have known for a long time that there is a powerful unconscious component in human experience. In 1821 in 'A Defence of Poetry' Shelley affirms that poetry 'acts in a divine and unapprehended manner, beyond and above consciousness' (1966: 423). But the unconscious in the psychoanalytic sense had to be discovered, to be analysed and evidenced in ways that might claim to be scientific. This began effectively when Freud, having qualified as a doctor, pursued his interest in neurology, by going to Paris in 1885, to the hospital of Salpêtrière where he studied with J.-M. Charcot. Charcot was using hypnosis to work on hysteria.

The existence of hypnosis is very well attested, a state in which an individual's consciousness is 'put to sleep' though they continue to respond to questions and commands. The idea of hysteria comes from the Greek for womb (*hysteron*) and names a malady supposed to give women hysterical symptoms. These were reinterpreted by Freud in a diagnosis he applied to men as well as women.

In a general sense hysteria refers to a psychosomatic symptom, a physical effect without a physical cause. A patient treated by Freud's colleague, Joseph Breuer, and written up as 'Anna O.' suffered from: a squint, feelings that the walls of the room were falling over, headaches, paralysis in the muscles of the neck which stopped her moving her head, loss of feeling and some loss of movement in the right arm (1973–86, vol 3: 75). Yet there was nothing physically wrong with her. And apparently all the symptoms were cured.

Breuer and Freud put forward the hypothesis that hysteria was caused by a traumatic experience which had become 'repressed' by passing into 'the unconscious' (both terms were introduced for the first time in this context, see, ibid: 61, 100). If they could get the patient to confront the terrible memory the symptoms disappeared – in Anna O.'s case a dream she had had while nursing her father that a black snake came out of the wall and tried to bite the sick man. The problem was to get them to remember ideas which were locked away from consciousness, and for this they turned to hypnosis. Later, Freud found it just as effective to ask the patient to associate ideas freely while he himself sat out of sight and took a neutral position. Anna O. christened psychoanalysis 'the talking cure' (ibid: 83) because it worked on, and through, spoken language and meanings.

While symptoms of the kind Freud and Breuer treated were not unusual at the end of the nineteenth century, they seem less common today. Possibly today hysteria is more likely to take the form of anorexia and bulimia. Freud, in fact, remarks that at the time of puberty some girls can begin to express 'an aversion to sexuality by means of anorexia' (1973–86, vol 9: 248). Psychological problems centred on food seem to be much more prevalent today. An advertisement for The Centre for Eating Disorders (*Guardian*, 18 June 1998) offers help for 'Compulsive Eating – Bingeing – Vomiting – Laxative Abuse – Overweight – Underweight – Fear of Food – Obsessive Exercising'.

DREAMS

Freud says the interpretation of dreams is '*the royal road*' to understanding the unconscious (1973–86, vol 4: 769). So here is a dream to start with:

> And he dreamed, and behold a ladder set up on the earth, and the top of it reached to heaven: and behold the angels of God ascending and descending it.

This is Jacob's dream from *Genesis*: 28. Dreaming, that mysterious and absolutely private mental activity which happens when you're asleep, has always been recognised as profoundly significant for human affairs and dreams mostly interpreted as prophesying the future. Freud would lead us towards a more earthy account of Jacob's ascent to heaven. 'Steps, ladders or staircases', he suggests in listing dream symbols, 'walking up or down them, are representations of the sexual act' (1973–86, vol 4: 472).

The 871 pages of *The Interpretation of Dreams* makes up one of the great, large books of our century, like Joyce's *Ulysses* or Pynchon's *Gravity's Rainbow*. Freud's whole story of the unconscious is in it. It is full of long, beautiful, complex and entirely plausible dreams (plausible, that is, because they're like the dreams we have), 47 dreamed by Freud and 176 dreamed by others, including the dream of Irma's injection, the 'phenyl-magnesium-bromide' dream, the supper of smoked salmon, the seal-like creature coming up through a trap-door, the girl in the white dress. From this treasury I have chosen one very short example. The youngest member of a family had this dream first at four years old and again repeatedly after that:

> A whole crowd of children – all her brothers, and sisters, and cousins of both sexes – were romping in a field. Suddenly they all grew wings, flew away and disappeared.
>
> (ibid: 353)

The trick is to discard all the ethical and moral sentiments of waking life and look for the pay-off: in imagining this little narrative what's in it for the dreamer? Let me invite readers to try out their psychoanalytic intuitions on this before moving on.

Those with brothers and sisters can usually recognise this text as motivated by sibling rivalry, acting out a wish that all the girl's relations would die so that, as Freud puts it, 'our little baby-killer was left alone' (ibid: 354), the sole object for her parents' attention. The most striking thing about a dream – if you remember it – is that though it evidently means something, it doesn't try to say anything to anyone. The opposite, in fact. A dream wants to remain *not understood*. All dreams are different; some are 'coherent, witty even, or fantastically beautiful' while others are 'confused, feeble-minded' or 'positively crazy' (1973–86, vol 1: 119–20). But all dreams camouflage their significance by being made up of concrete *visual* images jumbled together into a narrative.

Words do sometimes occur in dreams but, if they do, Freud says, they count not for what they say but the associations they carry. A woman dreamed that her husband said '*This will end in a general "Maistollmütz"*' (1973–86, vol 4: 404). Freud shows that what counts about this nonsense word is not anything that it means but that, like a term in a joke or a slip, it has associated connotations, including '*mais*' (maize), '*toll*' (mad), '*mannstoll*' (nymphomania), '*Meissen*' (porcelain bird), '*Miss*' (English: 'Miss') and '*mies*' (Yiddish: 'disgusting').

Dreams consist of '*the transformation of a thought into an experience*' (161), into what Freud elsewhere refers to as a 'thing-presentation', which, like the cinema, is made up of 'moving pictures'. Once again here we face the 'inner speech' problem. My dreams are visual and I assume yours are too. But the moment either of us tells someone about one it isn't an actual *dreamed* dream any more but a public representation of it in outer speech.

The inconsequential narrative of a dream which you may remember when you wake up is its *manifest* content. This, so Freud argues, takes the form it does so as to disguise the *latent* content of the dream, which expresses a wish. If the little baby-killer does want her siblings and relations dead, her dream doesn't say so explicitly but implies it with the delicate idea that 'they all grew wings' and 'flew away' – for good. Freud proposes that this disguise or censorship in dreams is maintained by four effects. First there is the representation in images. Then there is displacement in which important meanings appear only in an apparently trivial or marginal form (dying expressed as 'growing wings'). Ideas are condensed and superimposed on each other – it looks as though butterflies in the field the children were playing in turn into the angels which fly away. Finally, dreams are censored by the conscious mind by being cast into coherent speech if they are to be reported.

There are two main procedures to interpreting dreams and look for the desire hidden in the narrative. One is to consider the dream in the context of the dreamer's own life, using for example the method of free association to suggest what it might mean to them. If someone else had the dream '*A whole crowd of children*' it would have a different meaning. Second, dreams have a typical form and take part in that shared system of images and meanings Freud points to in fairytales, myths, jokes and so on.

Freud actually takes the risk of offering a list of dream symbols, both in *The Interpretation of Dreams* and sixteen years later in his *Introductory Lectures on Psychoanalysis*. This should not be applied in any mechanical way, since, as I have indicated, the dream belongs to the dreamer after all. But it's often helpful to keep the catalogue in mind, and it is surprising how often these symbols are unexpectedly confirmed. Here are some equivalences he suggests (see 1973–86, vol 1: 186–99; vol 4: 470–77):

> a necktie – penis: a tie is a long, dependent object peculiar to men; Freud remarks that unlike the physical organ a tie 'can be chosen according to taste' (1973–86, vol 4: 473)

> umbrella – penis (see, perhaps, the famous sequence from the Hollywood film, *Singing in the Rain?*)

> boxes and wood, chests, wooden boxes – women: and pianos? as in the film *The Piano* or Diana Ross's song about her 'old piano'?

> snakes – too easy: in 1916 Freud also mentions airships as having the same meaning

> flying – sexual excitement, an erection: being able to go up and stay up, like Superman

> landscapes – 'invariably the genitals of the dreamer's mother' (ibid: 524): all those paintings in the art galleries showing beautiful hills, lush valleys and fertile plains?

> a house – the individual's own body

> departure – dying

> flame – the male genital: and the fireplace 'its female counterpart', confirmed in the English male vulgarism that you don't look at the mantelpiece when you are stoking the fire

It is tempting (and often fun) to read off the symbols in text, to strip away the apparent meaning or manifest content and try to reveal the real meaning or latent content underneath. Freud warns against analysts who do just this, who ignore the complete dream-work in which manifest and latent have been worked together:

> They seek to find the essence of dreams in their latent content and in so doing they overlook the distinction between the latent dream-thoughts and the dream-work. At bottom, dreams are nothing other than a particular *form* of thinking, made possible by the conditions of the state of sleep.
>
> (1973–86, vol 4: 650, fn.)

Dreams are not the unconscious, the latent content is not the unconscious. Dreams are *one way* in which the unconscious speaks, 'a particular form of thinking' expressed in a specific form of representation.

Another is art. As will be discussed later, novels, films, poems, songs and paintings are like dreams except that they don't come with a dreamer attached. Rather, they are 'out there', in public discourse, until someone becomes attached to them.

SLIPS AND MISTAKES IN EVERYDAY LIFE

The unconscious is active all the time, not just when you're asleep. In one of his most popular and widely translated books, *The Psychopathology of Everyday Life* (1901), Freud looked at mistakes that we all make all of the time to show how they're not always mistakes. In fact, they may successfully act out an unconscious wish which consciously we might be ashamed of or deny. This is one area of Freud's analysis which has become pretty familiar since 1901 and I can be brief.

If you bump into somebody in the street or accidentally drop the ugly vase your aunt gave you it's because, unconsciously, you want to. If you forget the name of somebody you know perfectly well, or fail to recognise them at a party, it's because you want to (probably because you really wish they would grow wings and fly away). You can make mistakes with numbers or figures. One of Freud's typically sardonic stories (1973–86, vol 5: 285) concerns an over-cautious young man who finally proposed marriage to the woman he loved and then on the tram home alone found he had bought *two* tickets. Six months later, still wondering if he'd done the right thing, he got on a tram with his newly-wed partner and bought only *one* ticket.

Fiddling with things has an unconscious component, such as 'fingering one's beard', 'scribbling with a pencil that one happens to be holding' or 'jingling coins in one's pocket' (1973–86, vol 5: 250). But the most justly famous – and entertaining – way in which the unconscious intrudes into everyday life takes the form of verbal slips. A lot of innocent fun can be had if you listen to what people actually say and disregard what you know they're trying to say (just as people deny the sexual meaning of symbols, they often make verbal mistakes but nobody notices them).

1 I heard a nervous lecturer give a talk in which every time he referred to this 'seminar' he actually said 'scimitar'.
2 At her wedding in 1977, on television watched by a quarter of the world's population, Diana Spencer had to *repeat* the words of the Archbishop of Canterbury, 'Do you take Charles Philip etc. etc. to be your lawfully wedded husband?'. In fact she said 'Philip Charles . . .' (preferring the father to the son?).
3 On 6 May 1983 George Bush, then Vice-President of the United States, addressing a college in Southern Idaho, referred to his relationship with the President, Ronald Reagan:

> For seven-and-a-half years I've worked alongside him, and I'm proud to be his partner. We've had triumphs, we've made mistakes, we've had sex . . .
> [*audience laughter*]

Setbacks, we've had setbacks.

[*pause*]

I feel like the javelin competitor who won the toss and elected to receive.

(*New Statesman*, 27 May 1983)

4 In 1994 the then Chancellor of the Exchequer, Kenneth Clark, was asked how many jobs his welfare-to-work measures would create. Without pause he replied, 'I have not set a target for how many votes it will create' (*Guardian*, 8 December 1994).

5 On the Sky lunchtime news on 12 July 1998, condemning the deaths of the three children murdered in his constituency, the Rev. Ian Paisley tried to say it 'was repulsive to all right-thinking people'. He actually said it 'was republic . . .' (half-way to 'republican') before correcting himself.

Mistakes can also occur at the typewriter or the word processor. Someone I know found he couldn't stop typing 'pricniple' instead of 'principle'. Hysterical symptoms and dreams each have a specific operation, as do verbal slips. They are, however, very like jokes since we may find something funny in them even if they aren't necessarily intended to be funny. A group of English actors was being interviewed after a wildly successful first-night in New York. Asked what they were going to do next the director said they were all off to 'The Waldorf Hysteria'. A slip or a joke? Either way 'it' (the unconscious) spoke.

JOKES

'And, as true as God shall grant me all good things, Doctor, I sat beside Salomon Rothschild and he treated me quite as his equal – quite familionairely' (1973–86, vol 6: 47): the first example in Freud's 'Jokebook' has two sides or aspects. There is a play on words ('familiar' and 'millionaire' combined into 'familionairely'); second, the point or meaning of the joke which Freud says is

'Rothschild treated me quite as his equal, quite familiarly – that is, so far as a millionaire can' (ibid: 48). It is crucial that the joke produces a meaning through 'indirect representation' (ibid: 114), by a play on words or ideas. And it is powerful evidence in favour of this account of the joke that paraphrase – such as that Freud gives of the 'millionaire' joke – annihilates the joke altogether. What paraphrase does is get rid of the 'fore-pleasure' for which the full joke is the 'end-pleasure'. This is a distinction that is also important in the effect of art and will be discussed shortly.

Freud analyses the origin of jokes in the pleasures of children and the means by which those pleasures may be kept alive in an acceptable form by grown-ups. There are four categories of joke: pleasure in nonsense; the jest; the innocent or non-tendentious joke; and finally the tendentious joke, the joke proper. Pleasure in nonsense is at work when the child repeats similar sounds (a pleasure still there for an adult when Frank Sinatra sings, 'Do Be, Do Be, Do'). In the jest the same pleasurable play is cast into some pretence of coherent meaning ('Why is a king like twelve inches?' 'Because he's a ruler'). Both non-tendentious and tendentious jokes work with a legitimate and coherent meaning but one which, through a play on words or ideas, makes indirect allusion to another meaning. In the non-tendentious joke this meaning is 'innocent', as when at the Tory party conference a few years back Mrs Thatcher said, 'You turn (U turn) if you want – the lady's not for turning' (with a play on *The Lady's Not for Burning*, the title of a play by Christopher Fry). Freud's own example is 'We must hang together or else we will hang separately' (ibid: 181).

The tendentious joke has a point or meaning, as in the 'familionairely' example, because it draws on forbidden material and allows expression to what otherwise would be inhibited: ideas which are obscene, aggressive, cynical, absurd, blasphemous. Adult jokes continue to function through indirect representation which is either verbal or conceptual. The *double entendre* is a good example of verbal play, as when Mercutio in *Romeo and Juliet* is asked what time it is and replies 'the bawdy hand of the dial is now upon the prick of noon'. This joke is even better if you know that 'dial' was Elizabethan slang for female genitals. On English television there is a gay comedian, Julian Clary, who specialises in finding homoerotic meanings in words it's impossible to avoid – 'up', 'down', 'in', 'out', 'hot', 'large', 'small', 'head', etc.

In conceptual play the normal categories of association are disturbed to produce a sentence which in itself is coherent but makes little sense, until, re-interpreted in another context, it reveals its inhibited implication. An example, though of a rather special kind, is the joke Freud puts at the end of the first part of the book:

> Two Jews met in a railway carriage at a station in Galicia. 'Where are you going', asked one. 'To Cracow', was the answer. 'What a liar you are!', broke out the other. 'If you say you're going to Cracow, you want me to believe you're going to Lemberg. But I know that in fact you're going to Cracow. So why are you lying to me?'

The complex play of ideas, as Freud explains, is that the second Jew is lying 'when he tells the truth and is telling the truth by means of a lie' (ibid: 161).

It's not the slightest bit funny to say that acquaintances who meet by accident often lie to each other, nor is it funny to say 'a clock face is round like a woman's vagina and the hand of a clock is like a willy'. It's what the joke mechanism *does* that releases an unconscious meaning for a moment and makes a joke fun. But only once. You can only enjoy a joke a second time if you tell it to someone who hasn't heard it so you can enjoy it again through them.

I don't want to leave Freud on jokes without adding a very unfunny reflection on the book on jokes. Published in 1905 it contains jokes, good and bad, mainly from the huge thesaurus of

Central European Jewish humour. That culture disappeared almost entirely during 'The Final Solution', in which Freud's four sisters, Rosa, Mitzi, Dolfi and Paula, were killed. As for Cracow, it is now Krakow in Poland and Lemberg is Lvov in the Ukraine. Freud escaped to England in June 1938. Waiting to leave he was interrogated by the Gestapo and afterwards made to sign a document saying they had treated him well. Freud signed – and added at the bottom, 'I can heartily recommend the Gestapo to anyone' (Jones, 1956–58, vol 3: 241).

ART

I will use a separate chapter to explore the process of the unconscious as it is active in the aesthetic text but I want to introduce the topic here, by referring to a 1908 essay by Freud, 'Creative Writers and Day-Dreaming'. For Freud the origins of art lie in childhood, in the free and unself-conscious way the child *plays*. Such play is a serious matter. The child knows it is pretending; in fact it's a condition of play that the child 'distinguishes it quite well from reality' (1973–86, vol 14: 132). I remember when my son was five and one of my daughters was seven they would earnestly play 'Action Man and Sindy'. Years later they told me they had very different ideas for the game – he wanted Sindy to be a Hell Goddess with a Megablaster while she wanted them to sit by the pool chatting.

Freud's view is that no-one ever willingly gives up a pleasure they have once enjoyed, rather we simply 'exchange one thing for another' so that what appears to be 'renunciation is really the formation of a substitute' (ibid: 133). As we grow up we simply stop acting out our play with toys and instead try to replace it by making up day-dreams.

It might seem attractive to use a different spelling to distinguish between conscious Fantasies and unconscious Phantasies (this is suggested by Isaacs 1948). However, Freud insists there is a clear continuity between phantasy in dreams, day-dreams and art which makes it impossible to draw a line between conscious fictions and unconscious effects – 'every single phantasy is the fulfilment of a wish' (1973–86, vol 14: 134), night-dreams in the same way as day-dreams. So the same spelling (from the German: *Phantasie*) is appropriate for both though there is the difference that phantasies in night-dreams are much more distorted. Even so, I'm going to stay with the spelling 'fantasy'.

Everyone has day-dreams, usually erotic or ambitious, or both, but are ashamed to speak of them. More than once I've reached this point in a seminar on 'Creative Writers', noticed a look of horror pass across students' faces and guessed immediately what they were thinking: 'Oh Christ! He's going to ask us to tell him our day-dreams'. I never do, because I would be obliged to tell my own. If you do confess your fantasies to other people they generally find them boring and embarrassing, because they are so obviously self-concerned. This is one reason it is so unpleasant to read someone's personal diary. The creative writer is different because they *can* make their fantasies public so other people can enjoy them.

How is this done? Freud's answer is consistent with his analysis of other instances of unconscious expression. Just as dreams disguise a latent wish in the manifest content and jokes depend on the mechanism of indirect statement, so art works with a specific means of representation. There are two moves. First, creative writers soften the self-concerned character of their 'egoistic day-dreams' by altering and disguising it, presenting it in plausible and seemingly impersonal form. Second, the writer 'bribes us by the purely formal – that is, aesthetic – yield of pleasure' which is offered in the presentation of the fantasies (ibid: 141). The formal effect provides fore-pleasure, which was just what the play of words or ideas did in the joke.

For those who've been brought up to think of novels and plays as Great Literature, Tolstoy and Shakespeare as semi-divine, and

Beauty as a spiritual experience which you just can't talk about, this theory must seem rather deflating. It is, in fact, very much part of Freud's general scientific and moral purpose to show that mysteries, such as Great Art, which have often over-awed people, have a fairly ordinary, material explanation.

Freud claims that art begins in the pleasures of childhood we all go through. However, in arguing that there is a continuity between the ordinary joys of playing 'Action Man and Sindy' and the most sublime works of Mozart and Beethoven, Freud manages to avoid *reducing* art to childishness. He recognises that the capacity to turn your day-dreams into *Hamlet* and *King Lear* resists analysis because it works with the formal properties of art. These remain, he says, the 'innermost secret' of art (ibid: 140).

CASE HISTORIES

For more than 40 years Freud and his family lived at 19 Bergstrasse in a posh suburb of Vienna, in a first-floor flat which contained a number of large rooms. It is reached by going up a long flight of stairs. When I walked up these in 1996 I had time to think of Freud's famous patient, Wolfman, who must have mounted slowly, wondering anxiously exactly what the next session would have in store. It is worth noting that Freud's patients, such as Ratman and Wolfman, get their pseudonyms not from fifties' Hollywood movies but from the animals with which they were obsessed. At the top of the stairs there is a hallway, a door which leads into the waiting room, and another door from there into the consulting room, complete with couch. On the other side a door leads directly into Freud's study where he could easily retreat for a couple of minutes, even if only to look out of the window at the trees in the courtyard.

The theory of the unconscious is supported by the analysis of dreams, jokes, everyday mistakes and art. But its main confirmation comes from the speech of the hundreds – thousands – of patients Freud listened to over the decades. I'm not going to discuss any of the long, fascinating and tangled case histories but rather one that is in some ways simpler and certainly more charming – Little Hans.

Freud did see Little Hans on a few occasions but the case was mostly recorded by the boy's father, a fan of psychoanalysis, who wrote down conversations with his son (since the father was the focus of the boy's anxieties this introduces something a bit creepy into the whole business).

Just before he was three Little Hans showed a lively interest in his 'widdler', on one occasion addressing his mother:

> HANS: 'Mummy, have you got a widdler too?'
> MOTHER: 'Of course. Why?'
> HANS: 'I was only thinking.'
>
> (1973–86, vol 8: 171)

Around the same time he saw a cow being milked and exclaimed 'Oh, look! there's milk coming out of its widdler' (ibid). At three-and-a-half, two things happened to him. His sister was born and he had an exchange with his mother when she found him with his hand on his penis:

> MOTHER: 'If you do that, I shall send for Dr A, to cut off your widdler. And what'll you widdle with?'
> HANS: 'With my bottom.'
>
> (ibid: 171)

On one occasion, at four-and-a-quarter, Hans was having a bath and his mother was powdering round his penis but taking care not to touch it. He asked her 'Why don't you put your finger there?' and she replied it would be 'piggish'. His response, laughing, was 'But it's great fun.' (ibid: 182).

Suddenly, at four-and-three-quarters, Hans changes. Coming back from one of his favourite places in Vienna he becomes frightened, starts to cry and confesses to his mother, '*I was afraid a horse would bite me*' (ibid: 187). His father tells him that he may have been frightened when he saw a horse's big widdler and adds 'Big animals have big widdlers, and little animals have little widdlers' (ibid: 196). Little Hans catches the ball thrown to him but only in a way that reveals his worries: 'my widdler will get bigger as I get bigger; it's fixed in, of course' (ibid: 196). His phobia is intensified and combined with the memory of a horse falling down in the street.

At this point Freud is ready for an interpretation. The biting horse represents Hans' father that he was afraid of 'precisely because he was so fond of his mother' (ibid: 204); but his fear of his father was also a fear *for* his father (the fallen horse) (ibid: 207), the two ideas linked because he thought 'the horse (his father) would bite him because of his wish that it (his father) would fall down' (ibid: 212, footnote). Freud told Little Hans that he shouldn't think his father was angry with him because he loved his mother – 'his father was fond of him in spite of it' (ibid: 204). Little Hans at once began to improve (ibid: 205) and by the age of five 'ceased to be afraid of horses' though, to his father's amusement, he became 'rather familiar' towards his father (ibid: 301). In a 'Postscript' Freud says he met Hans again when he was nineteen and he 'could remember nothing' of any of this (ibid: 304).

I have omitted whole chunks of the narrative, including Hans' flirtatious wish to 'coax' his mother, his comment that his baby sister's widdler is quite small but will grow, the giraffe and its widdler, the whole question of *lumpf*, biting his father, butting his father in the stomach (and getting smacked for it), the idea of threatening his father with a gun, that at one point his fear of horses turns round into a compulsion to look at them, how his father's moustache and glasses reappear in his fantasies as the thick black harness for a dray-horse's head. What is remarkable about

'Analysis of a Phobia in a Five-year-old Boy' is that here, carefully written down, is exactly the kind of thing young children go on and on about and which adults generally overlook. Once again, in the case histories 'it speaks'.

If even this relatively straightforward narrative can generate such a proliferation of complicated meanings, how much more so the cases of 'Wolfman' and 'Ratman'! Freud scored some fairly spectacular early successes in curing hysteria but this was not matched when the cases were more knotted and confused.

In a paper of 1937 somewhat ominously entitled 'Analysis Terminable and Interminable' Freud noted that sometimes therapy ended satisfactorily, in other cases it couldn't because 'absolute psychic health' is impossible (1953–74, vol 23, pp. 219–20). It looks as though the sheer self-contradictory inventiveness of the unconscious was able to outrun even his most attentive sleuthing. At the end of 'An Autobiographical Study' (1925) Freud writes:

> While it was originally the name of a particularly therapeutic method, it has now become the name of a science – the science of unconscious mental processes. By itself this science is seldom able to deal with a problem completely, but it seems destined to give valuable contributory help in the most varied regions of knowledge.
>
> (1973–86, vol 15: 255)

He does not advance strong claims here for the capacity of psychoanalysis to put patients right. More mutedly, he suggests that the science of the unconscious will have a general application in different areas.

2

THE UNCONSCIOUS IN FREUD AND LACAN

Hysteria, dreams, jokes, slips, art, case histories: from here on the going gets a bit tougher so it may be helpful to pause and pull together a few statements about the unconscious that have emerged from the material reviewed so far. The unconscious:

- is elsewhere, since censorship ensures it never appears directly but only indirectly, disguised, in traces;
- works with meanings, meanings so charged they can make a perfectly healthy arm seem paralysed;
- works with meanings which take specific forms of representation, different in jokes and dreams, for example;
- seeks pleasure, a demand often expressed in fantasy;
- is childish;
- has no interest in conventional morality or the ethical obligations of civilisation;
- can contradict itself (Little Hans feared horses and felt compelled to look at them).

Though this should clarify some things retrospectively, it is now necessary to introduce a complication. Freud in fact distinguishes between conscious, unconscious and *preconscious* systems (designated as *Cs.*, *Ucs.*, and *Pcs.*). The preconscious is really a sub-division of consciousness but cannot be classified along with consciousness because it consists largely of memory, including things we do without thinking about them, such as walking and driving a car. Something you actually have in your mind *now* obviously is conscious. Something you know but are not actually thinking about has to be somewhere else, where you can get hold of it when you want – the preconscious. Ideas from the preconscious can slip into the unconscious, though unconscious thoughts can only enter the preconscious if subject to the usual censorship. For example, if you can't remember the name of someone you know, it has temporarily slipped from the preconscious into the unconscious.

THE UNCONSCIOUS AND CHILDHOOD

The unconscious originates in infancy. We tend to think of new-born babies as fragile but they're not. Five days after the 1985 earthquake in Mexico City 58 babies were saved from the wreckage of a maternity ward. Babies are fiercely energetic and know exactly what they want, a quality William Blake dramatises brilliantly in his poem, 'Infant Sorrow':

> My mother groan'd! my father wept,
> Into the dangerous world I leapt;
> Helpless, naked, piping loud:
> Like a fiend hid in a cloud.
>
> Struggling in my father's hands,
> Striving against my swadling-bands,
> Bound and weary, I thought best
> To sulk upon my mother's breast.
>   (1966: 217)

Freud suggests that 'what we describe as our "character"' is based on the impressions which 'have had the greatest effect on us', that is, ones from our infancy and earliest youth (1973–86, vol 4: 689). That they are so important to us is shown by the fact that we almost completely forget them, just as Little Hans forgot the whole affair of the frightening horses. In dreams we revisit this world of infant joy and sorrow:

> *a wish which is represented in a dream must be an infantile one.* In the case of adults it originates from the *Ucs.*, in the case of children, where there is as yet no division or censorship between the *Pcs.* and the *Ucs.*, or where that division is only gradually being set up, it is an unfulfilled, unrepressed wish from waking life.
>
> (ibid: 705)

The division between conscious and unconscious is not there from the beginning but has to be developed. In the process of growing up it comes about as a *split* (German: *Spaltung*) between the two, the effect of which is to guarantee that what is present in the unconscious is actively excluded from consciousness. In this scheme the preconscious can act as an intermediary. Strictly speaking, this way of defining the split belongs to Lacan, and is something he developed from Freud's account of 'Splitting of the Ego in the Process of Defence' (1973–86, vol 11: 457 ff.).

In the psychoanalytic account it is this split which makes human society possible. If there is no unconscious, then there can be no opposition between nature and culture. First, the split is a necessary condition for the existence of culture and civilisation since it means that all those violent, appetitive, anti-social drives – the infant, 'like a fiend', 'piping loud' – can be relegated to another place, the unconscious.

Second, the dynamic of the split negotiates the relation between social and individual, between the personal, infantile demands that persist in us all through our lives and the obligations civilisation imposes on us. The unconscious allows us to internalise much of our society and carry it around with us, leaving consciousness to get on with it (more or less), especially the use of coherent speech. Theories which do not work with a contrast of conscious/unconscious have to assume some kind of direct, abrasive and unmediated join between social life on the one hand, and the individual body on the other.

In Freud's pessimistic view, to be human necessarily involves a loss. The split between conscious and unconscious is brought about through a great act of *renunciation*.

I grew up in the shadow of the Second World War and still find it hard to fly across the Channel without hearing a voice crackling on the intercom: 'Dutch coast ahead! From now on expect enemy fighters!'. After 1941 when the Americans joined the war they said they would bomb Germany in daylight to be sure of hitting the target (the RAF went on bombing at night though they couldn't hit anything except large cities). Before proper fighter cover was introduced in early 1944 the Americans were losing around 7 per cent of aircraft every mission (a complete tour was 24 missions). Day after day young men would climb into fragile aluminium cylinders packed with TNT and high-octane aviation fuel, then fly five miles above the earth in brilliant sunshine while being shot at by anti-aircraft batteries on the ground and enemy fighters in the air.

At the same time young women with bilingual abilities would volunteer to join Special Operations Executive and be parachuted into occupied territory to spy for the Allies. If caught they would suffer a slow, desolate and excruciating death under torture.

How can people do such things when every 'natural feeling' is crying out to stop you? For psychoanalysis the answer can only be in the renunciation of instinct and drive. Those extreme examples are intended to suggest that psychic forces even *stronger* than 'natural feelings' are needed to support civilisation (fighting

Nazism was definitely a defence of civilisation). What are these psychic forces? How is renunciation achieved? And what is renounced?

OEDIPUS

When he started treating cases of hysteria Freud had been struck by the fact that his patients wanted to forget something and that what they forgot was usually sexual. It was precisely on this point that he and his colleague Breuer parted company. Trying to solve the riddle of what might be the deepest motivations in human behaviour Freud, in 1897, came to appreciate insights that were in Sophocles' play, *Oedipus the King*, first performed in Athens around 427 BC.

Oedipus is brought up as the son of the ruler of Corinth until one day a prophet tells him he is destined to kill his father and marry his mother. He immediately leaves home. On the road he gets into a row with a man about right of way at a junction, and in the ensuing fight kills him. Arriving in Thebes he saves the city by solving the riddle of the Sphinx and is rewarded by being married to the queen, who has been recently widowed. It turns out that he was in fact a foundling, brought to Corinth as a baby, that the man killed at the junction was his father and the woman he has just married is – his mother. Oedipus blinds himself and goes into exile.

It is no accident that Freud's own father died in 1896, of natural causes, not at a road junction, a year or two before Freud started working seriously on *The Interpretation of Dreams*. He refers to Sophocles' play, especially to one point when Oedipus is worrying about the fate prophesied for him; his wife tries to reassure him:

> Many a man ere now in dreams hath lain
> With her who bare him.

(Freud 1973–86, vol 4: 366)

Freud reads this dream easily enough. 'It is', he says, 'the fate of all of us, perhaps, to direct our first sexual impulse towards our mother and our first hatred and our first murderous wish against our father' (ibid: 364). After discussing *Oedipus* Freud takes up Shakespeare's masterpiece, *Hamlet*, and confirms his understanding from that. Hamlet finds it hard to attack the man who has just married his mother because his step-father represents 'the repressed wishes of his own childhood' (ibid: 367).

How do women figure in the Oedipus situation? This is a topic properly for the next chapter but something needs to be said here. At first Freud thought that every little girl directs her first sexual impulse towards father and hates her mother. He soon realised that the feminine version was not simply a reverse of the masculine since little girls *also* direct their first sexual impulse towards the mother. Received opinion is that the world is simply divided into real men and and real women. But as we shall see, psychoanalysis thinks sexuality is much more complicated and uncertain than that.

From the start the human subject is divided. In the Oedipus complex the incestuous drive towards the mother is immediately matched by opposing forms of drive, expressed as the threat of castration from the father. This was a persistent theme in the story of Little Hans. The fundamental contradiction is bluntly stated by Jacques Lacan when he says that 'the Sovereign Good . . . which is the mother, is also the object of incest' and so 'a forbidden good' (1992: 70). *Oedipus* and *Hamlet* both present this conflict. Without meaning to, Oedipus does have intercourse with his mother and then feels so bad about it that he blinds himself; Hamlet is commanded to take revenge against his step-father by the Ghost of his own father but finds it almost impossible to kill the man who is making love with his mother. Freud remarks how 'every new arrival on this planet is faced by the task of mastering the Oedipus complex; anyone who fails to do so falls a victim to neurosis' (1973–86, vol 7: 149 fn.).

Oedipus and *Hamlet* are familiar classical examples, but since later on I will argue that the unconscious from the most ancient societies is still alive in the contemporary world, here is a contemporary example. In Howard Hawks's western, *Red River* (1948), John Wayne leads a cattle drive. Some of the cowboys he has recruited dispute his leadership, steal food and run off. When they are caught Wayne proposes to hang them. When they reply that the law might have something to say about this, he asserts, '*I'm the law*'. At this point the others gang up against him, stop the hanging, take his cows and leave him behind. His parting words are, 'I'll kill you – every time you turn round expect to see me.' There follows a very spooky scene in mist near a river at dusk when the cowboys try to sleep but keep jumping at shadows, pulling guns on each other, having nightmares. The dead father, the spectral father, is more potent than any live one.

The prohibition on incest is universal and specific to the species, although the particular persons forbidden as incestuous objects vary across different societies (see below pp. 148–50). This universality is one of the strongest pieces of evidence for the existence of the unconscious. The law against incest is an external social institution corresponding to the Oedipus complex in the unconscious.

CASTRATION

Freud notes that 'the blinding in the legend of Oedipus . . . stands for castration' (1973–86, vol 4: 522 fn.). Castration can be misunderstood, and there may well be good reasons people do their best to make a joke of it. In the first place no society would last very long if fathers *actually* castrated their sons. Second, the signifiers which represent castration are quite specific in that the process consists of a threat to the genitals, not something else. In reality this might not seem too bad; after all, worse things can happen to you. But in fantasy castration *is* the worst thing that can happen. I can experience the death of others but I cannot experience my own death since I won't be *there* to know about it. Freud asserts that 'the fear of death' is a 'development of the fear of castration' (1973–86, vol 11: 400). Nothing can be worse for us than the idea of losing our sexuality and capacity to love and be loved. In fact, it is a Christian commonplace that Hell is eternal deprivation of the love of God.

At the end of the most famous English novel of the century, Orwell's *Nineteen Eighty-Four*, Winston Smith's captors promise to take him to Room 101 and do 'the worst thing in the world' (1984: 228) to him. This consists of a cage with starving rats which can be released towards his face. He's told, 'they attack the eyes first . . . a common punishment in Imperial China' (ibid: 230). Is this the worst? Freud's Ratman is called this because he was preoccupied with 'a specially horrible punishment used in the East' (1973–86, vol 9: 47), also involving rats. They are directed not against the eyes but the anus. Is that worse? Well, in Freud's account the fantasy image of castration is worse still, absolutely the worst thing in the world, worse than death.

REPRESSION

Castration therefore cannot be borne by the conscious mind, and so it must be pushed away into the unconscious. It must be *repressed* and the unconscious is developed for that purpose. A brief answer to my earlier question, 'How could the brave young men and women in the Second World War face death in some of its most awful manifestations?', is that they repressed their fear of it, something that would have been impossible if they hadn't already at a younger age repressed the desire for the mother and its accompanying threat of castration. To be precise, it's the signifiers for them that are repressed. The process can be illustrated from this present discussion which, necessarily, has contained some atrocious material: death, torture, rats, incest, parricide. These ideas are endurable because they are only present in the conscious mind while the signifiers which represent the real fantasies attached to them are safely locked away in the unconscious.

But how does repression *begin* in any individual? As a follower of Darwin, Freud believed in the crucial role of genetics, a view supported by scientific common sense today. Even if you nurture a baby chimpanzee lovingly it does not grow up to be a human child. Software is not enough, you need the wiring as well. Freud therefore kept coming back to the idea that we inherit some of our ideas, preserving 'memories of what was experienced by our ancestors' (1973–86, vol 13: 346).

After all, the other animals do. A baby baboon will run in terror from a rope waggled in its face because it was born with the idea already in its head that snakes are very dangerous for baboons. Freud supposes that there is some degree of *primary repression*, that this is inherited, and that it provides a matrix for the individual's own repression to hook onto. Not only are certain signifiers denied entry to consciousness, they are also attracted to 'what was primally repressed' ('Repression', 1973–86, vol 11: 148). However, they are not simply fixed once and for all but are '*mobile*' in relation to each other (ibid: 151). Hidden away from the influence of consciousness, an idea can grow more profusely. It actively 'proliferates in the dark' (ibid: 148) as Freud puts it.

This being the case there is always likely to be 'a *return of the repressed*' (ibid: 154). Freud cites a medieval monk who was trying to get rid of sexual temptation by gazing on the image of the Crucifixion, when suddenly 'the image of a voluptuous, naked woman' appeared to him in the same crucified attitude (1973–86, vol 14: 60). Return of the repressed is familiar as a trope from Hollywood. Just when you think the danger is safely over and everyone's relaxing because the creature, whether it is a giant shark, alien, Freddie Kruger, or the Thing), has been finally eradicated, that's when it's most liable to stage a reappearance: the bloody hand coming out of the grave at the end of *Carrie*, Sigourney

Weaver thinking she has finally got rid of the alien when she escapes in her pod from the mother-ship, the missing body on the lawn at the end of *Halloween*. It's because the repressed returns as hysteria, symptoms, dreams and so on, that we have to turn to the hypothesis of the unconscious.

LAW, LANGUAGE AND SOCIETY

The Oedipus complex, incest, castration, repression: Deleuze and Guattari have complained that Freud's account is mechanical and reductive (Jacques Derrida (1987) makes a comparable accusation against Jacques Lacan). Taking the example of Freud's patient who saw a vision of wolves in a large tree outside his window (quoted in full on pp. 109–10) they claim Freud always comes back to one thing: 'the little scars, the little holes, become subdivisions of the great scar or supreme hole named castration; the wolves become substitutes for a single Father who turns up everywhere, or wherever they put him' (1987: 31). 'Kipling', they say, in the *Mowgli* stories, 'understood the call of the wolves, their libidinal meaning, better than Freud' (ibid: 31). Freud transforms complexity into simplicity, the multiplicities of the unconscious into a single figure, the Father: 'Oedipus, nothing but Oedipus' (ibid: 34).

I think there are basically two ways to respond to this objection. The first is put forward by Juliet Mitchell, who in 1974 published a very influential book, *Psychoanalysis and Feminism*. Mitchell argues that the 'Oedipus' system – the incestuous wish and threat of castration presided over by the father – is necessary to produce human society. This is a historical not eternal effect:

> To date, the father stands in the position of the third term that *must* break the asocial dyadic unit of mother and child. We can see that this third term will always need to be represented by something or someone.

> (1982: 23)

So, the dyadic unit of mother and child is asocial, would hold us back in nature, and it must be broken by something or someone, but not necessarily *the father*.

The second argument is already implied by Mitchell: the prohibition on incest comes to operate as the very model for law. The anthropologist, Claude Lévi-Strauss (see 1969), affirms that what matters about the incest taboo is not its content, that it forbids incest, but that it prohibits a natural feeling. It thus introduces a *general* opposition between nature and culture, transgression and law, desire and the renunciation of desire.

I will explore the work of Jacques Lacan more fully later on. Let me anticipate that discussion by saying here that for Lacan, like Lévi-Strauss, what counts is not so much the prohibition on incest but the *fact* of prohibition itself. Lacan submits that it is language, the order of the signifiers, which imposes castration or lack as the infant (Latin: *infans*, 'not speaking') develops into a child, a speaking subject. He finds warrant for this view in Freud's extraordinary discussion of the so-called *fort/da* game.

This is a game Freud's grandson invented for himself at the age of one-and-a-half and which Freud analyses in *Beyond the Pleasure Principle* (1973–86, vol 11: 283–86). The child had learned only a few words and some sounds understood by those around him. He was 'greatly attached to his mother' (ibid: 284) though didn't cry when she left him. But, as Freud describes in 'Creative Writers and Day-Dreaming', he had learned to play. He had a wooden reel with a piece of string tied round it; he held the string and threw the reel into his cot, so that it disappeared. As he did this he went 'o-o-o-o', which his mother agreed was the German word '*fort*' ['gone']. Then he pulled the reel back with a 'joyful "*da*" ["there"]' (ibid.). This, the *fort/da* game, he 'repeated untiringly' (ibid.).

A lot of people with small children have been irritatingly caught up in similar forms of play. The child in its pram throws a fluffy toy onto the ground, you bend down, pick it up and give it back.

Then it gets thrown out again, to be picked up once more and returned. In my experience parents get tired of this one long before the child does.

Freud's interpretation of the *fort/da* game is that the little boy is compensating himself for the 'renunciation' he has made 'in allowing his mother to go away' by himself 'staging the disappearance and return of the objects within his reach' (ibid: 285). However, what preoccupies Freud, and chimes in with his broader concerns in *Beyond the Pleasure Principle*, is why the boy would want to repeat his 'distressing experience' (ibid.). Freud suggests a series of answers. Playing the *fort/da* game shifts the child from a position of passive to active; it acts out a drive for mastery; it allows the child to imagine revenge on his mother for going away – the same child sometimes threw a toy he was angry with on the floor exclaiming, ' "Go to the fwont!" ' (ibid.) like his father who had been sent away to fight at the front in the First World War. As Freud remarks, the boy 'was far from regretting his absence' (ibid: 286).

Taking these hints about how a loss can seem to be mastered in fantasy and in words, Lacan elaborates them. He proposes that being able to speak affords a degree of control to the child who has learned to do it. But in a quite new development Lacan claims that language *itself* acts like castration in transforming the infant into the child; it brings about the very loss the child tries to deal with. 'The symbol', says Lacan, 'manifests itself first of all as the murder of the thing' (1977a: 104). The symbol (word, image or sign) can stand for the real thing; but by being named the thing loses its self-definition, its simple capacity to be itself. Once named it could be named in *some other way*.

What the infant loses by entering language is its own direct self-identity, just being itself, as it seemed to be in the asocial, dyadic relation with the mother. But the child, now a speaking subject, has acquired something to try to make up for this loss – language and human social intercourse. In this account language breaks the bond between mother and infant, propelling a move from nature into culture. Lacan's different conception of the unconscious will be further explored in later chapters.

FREUD AND THE UNCONSCIOUS

The nature of the unconscious is summed up in Freud's essay of that title (1915). Conscious is split from unconscious which is itself divided between a repressed unconscious and the preconscious, the place of our 'latent memories' (1973–86, vol 11: 168). The unconscious in Freud's summary has four characteristics:

1 '*exemption from mutual contradiction*': opposed wishes can co-exist in the unconscious, as does Little Hans' fear *of* his father alongside his fear *for* his father, as do the desire for and prohibition of incest; this effect of living with contradictions is enormously enhanced by the way the unconscious speaks in images rather than words;

2 '*primary process*': energies in the unconscious are not fixed but mobile, liable to recombine into new configurations in an active process like that in which meanings are displaced and superimposed in dreams; the unconscious 'is alive' (ibid: 194), and this makes repressed material likely to return to consciousness in some form;

3 '*timelessness*': the processes of the unconscious are not 'ordered temporally', are 'not altered by the passage of time' (ibid: 191), in fact have no reference to time at all (this is an issue we will need to come back to);

4 '*replacement of external by psychical reality*': the unconscious essentially seeks pleasure and since it has little need to have regard for reality it will readily express itself in wishes and fantasies.

'Word-presentations' and 'thing-presentations'

The question that most concerns Freud in his paper is how exactly ideas are transposed between the unconscious and the conscious mind. For an answer he turns to something that is important in all the classic instances of the unconscious to which I have referred: representation. Freud has already noted that the 'literal' meaning of words in dreams does not matter as much as their associations (the woman who dreamed that her husband said, '*This will end in a general "Maistollmütz"*'). It is well know that even the most abstract words originate with and may be made to recall concrete connotations. In any case, the opposition between the literal meaning of a word or phrase and its connotations depends very much on how it is used. Many jokes depend upon taking a word meant literally and revealing another meaning in it: Mercutio's 'prick of noon', which literally means 'point of noon', can also mean 'penis'.

With this effect in mind Freud turns to the behaviour of some neurotic patients who used words in a similar way. For example, one young male patient had withdrawn from social life because of his bad skin. He felt that he had blackheads and deep holes in his face. Finding that a hole appeared whenever he got rid of a blackhead he reproached himself for ruining his skin by (in his words) '"constantly fiddling about with his hand"' (ibid: 205). Freud's interpretation is that pressing out the content of the blackheads was 'a substitute for masturbation' and the cavity which then appeared represented the female genitals and threat of castration, which was the very threat provoked by his masturbation.

The implication of the example is this: the two meanings (masturbation, squeezing blackheads) are very different, but the patient's phrase, 'constantly fiddling about with his hand', brings them together because it can suggest both, and this opens a path to the unconscious. Freud's hypothesis is that conscious and unconscious may be characterised generally by different kinds of representation; these he refers to, a little awkwardly, as 'word-presentations' and 'thing-presentations'.

Thus 'the conscious presentation comprises the presentation of the thing plus the presentation of the word belonging to it, while the unconscious presentation is the presentation of the thing alone' (ibid: 207). When we think about an idea it comes into our minds as a word but at the same time it is also present in the unconscious as a 'thing'. But presentation as a word blocks the appearance of the thing-presentation. The unconscious refuses to translate itself into words, and if it does, expresses itself only ambiguously and indirectly by finding other meanings beside the literal meaning.

It would be convenient if one could say the word-presentations were verbal signifiers and thing-presentations visual signifiers. But the issue is not as simple as that. Freud consistently uses thing-presentations to refer to the concrete visual images that dominate dreams. But we can also treat 'words as things' by focusing on 'the *sound* of the word instead of upon its meaning' (1973–86, vol 6: 167–68). The distinction seems to be that word-presentations are signifiers nailed down by the conscious mind to a *single* meaning, a denotation; in thing-presentations, whether visual or verbal, the signifier opens onto a *plurality* of meaning, as in a phrase like 'fiddling about with his hand', and so onto unconscious possibilities. Freud remarks that in 'a serious use of words' (ibid: 168) we restrict ourselves to a single, precise meaning, holding ourselves back from playing with variable meanings, a pleasure we are free to enjoy in puns, jokes and slips.

The contrast between word-presentations and thing-presentations helps to explain Freud's view that the unconscious is timeless. He gives the example of a patient who says to him:

> 'You ask who this person in the dream can be. It's *not* my mother'.

Freud comments that we at once emend this to, 'So it *is* his mother' (1973–86, vol 11: 437). He regards the capacity to negate or deny like this (the word *Verneinung* means both 'negation' and 'denial') as peculiar to consciousness; the capacity to distinguish 'it is' and 'it is not' are possible only in the abstract and logical mode of words and language.

Not so in the unconscious. It contains 'only contents' (1973–86, vol 11:190) without negation, denial or absence. It presents itself mainly in visual signifiers and this leads to the question: how do you produce an image which means 'not'? An image called up to represent 'not' or 'absent' will, necessarily, itself be *present* concretely as an image. All there can be are juxtapositions, contradictions and opposed meanings which try to cancel each other. And dreams casually merge remote childhood memories with what happened yesterday. Since everything can only be present in the unconscious without regard to temporal sequence Freud believes the unconscious is timeless.

I suspect that it is the affinity between the unconscious and visual signifiers which explains the passion with which Western culture has embraced the pleasures of seeing. There is, first, the tradition of oil-painting and perspective representation introduced at the time of the Renaissance, and later, deriving from this, photography, leading in the twentieth century to 'moving pictures', images in narrative sequence. In the 1920s the Surrealists thought they could use this new visual technology to present the unconscious *directly*, as it is, by showing images such as a woman's eye cut by a razor, ants coming out of a man's hand, or a female breast turning into a buttock when caressed. But if they thought they could side-step censorship they misread Freud. In the cinema viewers are fully conscious and simply introduce conscious inhibitions on the material for themselves, for example by dismissing it all as 'just more Surrealist crap'.

Because it always justifies its images with a believable narrative, thus satisfying conscious censorship, Hollywood cinema has been much more effective in evoking the intense, seductive and hallucinatory power of the visual signifier, in ways which are both attractive and compellingly repulsive. Readers can fill in their own examples but mine would include: Gene Kelly dancing and singing in the rain; *Psycho*, after the shower murder when the blood is followed as it runs into the round drain which, in close up, occupies the whole screen until there is a cut to the eye of the dead Janet Leigh (an image of absence?); the first sequence of *Apocalypse Now* ('It is the end') with its superimposed images of jungle/ hotel room/ napalm/ inverted head/ helicopter/ ventilator fan, resolved when Martin Sheen goes to the window and exclaims, 'Shit, Saigon, I'm still only in Saigon'.

LACAN AND THE UNCONSCIOUS

This discussion of signifiers used with a single, primary, literal meaning, and signifiers opening onto several meanings is an appropriate moment to introduce Lacan's notion of the unconscious. Freud's account of the unconscious is essentially an analysis of *meaning*. Under the impact of contemporary linguistics, particularly the work of Saussure and Jakobson, Lacan undertook to follow Freud by rethinking the unconscious in relation to language. Hence Lacan's famous principle, 'the unconscious is structured like a language' (e.g. 1977b: 203, 1993: 167).

Freud argues that:

cs = word-presentations + thing-presentations

but that:

ucs = only thing-presentations.

This formulation implies that the means of representation alone is enough to split conscious and unconscious. In this view the unconscious has become, as it were, functionally unconscious because you can't be conscious *only* of thing-presentations without the words. It is not actively repressed but really more like Freud's preconscious. In early Freud the unconscious is almost a kind of agency while in Lacan it appears more as an effect, in the gaps which *interrupt* consciousness.

Lacan turns away from Freud's view of the unconscious as a Hell below where we hide away all the big, bad beasties of our repressed desires (alive and, as Freud says, proliferating 'in the dark', 1973–86, vol 11: 148). For Lacan 'the unconscious is neither primordial nor instinctual' (1977a: 170), rather it is something that happens when coherent language becomes dislocated.

Saussure distinguished between the level of the shaped *sound* of a word (the signifier) and the meaning attached to it (the signified); together signifier and signified form a completed sign. When we are talking or writing our own language we overlook its signifiers; we think we just 'express' ourselves, making outside what comes from inside, apparently without mediation. Lacan's view is that, from the time we enter language, we always have to 'pass through the defiles of the signifier' (1977a: 264). Hence his definition of a signifier:

> The definition of a signifier is that it represents a subject not for another subject but for another signifier. This is the only definition possible of the signifier as different from the sign. The sign is something that represents something for somebody, but the signifier is something that represents a subject for another signifier.
>
> (1972a: 194)

This seems paradoxical. Surely the job of a signifier is trivial, simply a mechanical means by which meaning is transmitted? Not for Lacan in his reading of Saussurian linguistics.

Signifiers are based in phonemes and, according to Saussure, phonemes are defined in their relation to each other – thus in

Modern English /p/ is defined by contrast with /b/ and /t/ with /d/ and so on (including the vowels). Phonemes:

> are characterised not, as one might think, by their own positive quality but simply by the fact that they are distinct. Phonemes are above all else, opposing, relative, and negative entities.
>
> (Saussure 1959: 119)

Phonemes and signifiers relate in the first place to *each other* in an autonomous system which has no interest whatsoever in meaning: signifier 1 + signifier 2 + signifier 3. The subject must first enter this system in which signifiers relate to each other independently of the subject (representing a subject for another signifier) *before* there can be 'communication' through the completed sign (signifier + signified). The sign, communication, to 'represent something for somebody', does indeed take place but it is a secondary effect.

When you are talking or writing you think about what you are saying and can't at the same time be aware of the *sounds* you are using even though meaning depends on them. Lacan would identify the completed sign as the place of consciousness, and the signifier as the place where the unconscious operates. It makes conscious meaning possible by being *excluded* from it.

For Lacan the split between conscious and unconscious is like the bar which separates signifier and signified:

S
—
s

where big S is the signifier and little s the signified underneath it (1977a: 149). The subject appears present to itself in the signified and completed sign, but is lacking or barred from itself in the signifier.

To produce coherent meaning language has at its disposal two dimensions. There is the linearity of the order of words as they develop in time; and there is choice at any point of selecting a word from the reservoir of possible meanings. In Modern English 'Do bats eat cats?' produces a different meaning from 'Do cats eat bats?' because there is a different order; 'Do cats eat rats' produces a different meaning because 'rats' has been selected instead of 'bats'. Roman Jakobson rethinks the ideas of linearity and substitution in terms of metonymy and metaphor (see 1956: 55–82); Lacan draws on this to explain how unconscious significances can cross the bar to emerge alongside or even within coherent meaning (see 1977a: 156–59).

In metonymy a possible signifier already in the linear chain crosses the bar by producing an unintended signified. There's a crude old rugby ditty (sung to the tune of Mozart's *Eine kleine Nachtmusik*) in which the word 'Arsehole!' is repeated twice until it turns into the innocuous sentence: 'A soldier I will be'. In metaphor the signifier accidentally suggests a meaning that becomes associated with, or substituted for, the intended meaning (so 'prick of noon' means 'point of noon' but also 'penis').

A sentence unfolds temporally, along a line; reading or hearing it word by word we anticipate possible meanings and then further on try to lay them aside if we find they're not intended. Lacan refers to the point when sense seems to be resolved or buttoned down as an 'anchoring point' ('*point de capiton*' (ibid: 303)). An example would be the pause introduced after 'A sol . . .' in my rude example, because it turns 'A soldier' into something else. This place of apparently completed sense provides a conscious meaning but only temporarily, until some new sentence develops.

What matters for Lacan is that coherent sense can never exclude the effects of metonymy and metaphor. Unintended meanings are always excited and have to be actively denied. There is always a 'sliding of the signifier under the signified' (ibid: 160), there is no set of terms which cannot produce an 'improper' meaning. Here 'it speaks': the unconscious is 'a play of the signifier' that appears in 'dreams, slips of the tongue, witticisms, or symptoms' (1977b: 130).

Meaning is always *particular* in a particular context, but language is by nature *universal*, combining and re-using the same stock of terms from one context to another. When anyone intends to say anything there is always an overwhelming excess of meaning that has to be denied. For Lacan this constitutes the basis for the unconscious. He introduces the term 'Imaginary' for the state in which the subject, as it were, overlooks the signifier and finds meaning apparently present to consciousness; and the term 'Symbolic' for the organisation of signifiers which makes this possible and of which it is an effect (you can't have a signified without a signifier).

SOME QUALIFICATIONS

There are 24 volumes of Freud's work in the *Standard Edition*; Lacan's annual *Seminar* ran for 27 years. So, inevitably, my summary will not be complete. This section is a kind of appendix to the chapter in which I will at least make some gesture towards complications, particularly complications caused by change and development in Freud's thinking.

1 So far I have treated Freud as though he basically worked with an opposition between conscious and unconscious (and preconscious). In fact increasingly from the 1914 paper, 'On Narcissism: an Introduction', which recognised how far the ego was rooted in the unconscious, and decisively in *The Ego and the Id* in 1923, Freud revised his map or model of the psychic apparatus, his 'topography'. He did not give up conscious and unconscious but now gave priority to three different agencies, ego, id and super-ego (these are the translator's terms; Freud actually writes 'I', 'it' and 'over-I'). The id is the reservoir of libido or psychic energy which is tapped off in the form of the ego and the super-ego. In this revised conception the super-ego now has a separate task of performing as the voice of conscience and censorship.

2 The unconscious, the id, seeks pleasure and avoids unpleasure. But it causes a problem for the unconscious if there is any '*replacement of external by psychical reality*'. A real sexual partner is more satisfying than an imaginary one but how can the unconscious distinguish between them? The ego is developed as a system which discriminates between real and unreal so that the unconscious does not waste its time on hallucinations but can achieve real gratification, even if it is deferred.

Such was Freud's view when he wrote about the pleasure-principle and reality-principle in 1911. In 1920, after the First World War, his views had changed and he now acknowledges something *Beyond the Pleasure Principle* (the title of his book of that year, see 1973–86, vol 11). It is widely agreed that these 70 pages are the most suggestive and visionary he ever wrote. It is also felt that the argument is either finally incoherent or that we just don't properly understand it. For this reason I only mention it here, very cursorily.

Septimus, the shell-shocked soldier in Virginia Woolf's novel, *Mrs Dalloway*, written just after the Great War, keeps on seeing the same nightmare event all over London: another soldier, Evans, is running towards him; Septimus shouts 'Keep back'; but Evans keeps coming and is blown to pieces, as Septimus knows he will be. Partly because of evidence that shell-shocked soldiers did not just seek pleasure, but rather that they endlessly and desperately repeated the painful trauma which had damaged them, Freud looks beyond the pleasure principle. The trouble is that what he sees there is more than one thing: a compulsion not to seek pleasure but to repeat; a drive towards mastery; a drive to return to an earlier state (including the state you were in five minutes before you were conceived, i.e. not there at all, i.e. dead).

Freud's account of the two great forms of drive, narcissism and sexuality, leaned on Darwin's account of the instincts for reproduction and survival. Along the same lines Freud now reasons that if nature has programmed into us an instinct whose task is 'to lead organic life back into the inanimate state' (1973–86, vol 11: 380), then there may well be something corresponding to this instinct at the level of drive, a death drive in fact. This leads Freud to revise his former division of drive into two main forms, so-called 'ego-libido' and 'object-libido'. He now groups these together as life drives or Eros. Opposed to them, in a new binary with two terms, is Thanatos or the death drive. After 1920 Freud comes to regard the death drive as mixed in with most things people do.

This chapter began by distinguishing between instinct and drive. Freud inherited from Darwin a legacy in which self-preservation was contrasted with reproduction (corresponding to the 'common, popular distinction between hunger and love', 1973–86, vol 11: 70). This suggested to him an initial division between the forms of drives aimed at self-love, which I shall discuss in the next chapter, and those seeking sexual satisfaction, which I shall discuss in the one after that.

3

THE UNCONSCIOUS
AND THE 'I'

Twenty years ago most people who could not cope with life were looked after in an 'asylum' – now they have been 'returned to the community', the streets, that is. An unprecedented number of disturbed individuals wander about talking to themselves or shouting at some invisible enemy. Usually their hairstyle is distinctive – long, matted, dirty, sticking up in clumps over the head.

Not looking after your hair is a sign of despair and self-hatred, looking after it shows a necessary self-respect. Tony Adams, England and Arsenal defender and reformed alcoholic, said that in his drinking days he would wake up and pull on a pair of jeans he'd peed in the night before but which had dried out (*Guardian* 5 September, 1998). This was not a sign of psychic health. People use the word 'narcissistic' to criticise someone for excessive self-concern but a degree of self-love, corresponding to the instinct for survival, accounts for much that is best in civilisation. We could not manage without it.

The ego offers positive forms of pleasure. In the dystopian

future of Ray Bradbury's story *Fahrenheit 451* all books are forbidden because they make people unhappy by making them think about themselves. As they do, at least in the 1966 film of the book. At one point Oskar Werner reads the opening of Dickens' *David Copperfield*:

> Whether I shall turn out to be the hero of my own life, or whether that station will be held by anybody else, these pages must show. To begin my life with the beginning of my life, I record that I was born (as I have been informed and believe) on a Friday, at twelve hour at night. It was remarked that the clock began to strike, and I began to cry, simultaneously.

Oskar Werner himself cannot stop crying as he reads because he realises what he's been missing. Here lie the pleasures of the ego, consciousness, the individual's inner world, bodily control, self-awareness, an effect of mastery, the ability to distinguish fact from fiction. Modern democracy, voting, opinion polls, the civil rights of the individual – all are supported by the pleasures of narcissism.

THE EGO

'A unity comparable to the ego cannot exist in the individual from the start; the ego has to be developed' (Freud, 'On Narcissism', 1973–86, vol 11: 69). Unlike the soul of a Christian, Freud does not think that the ego is born into you once and for all but comes about in a material process. One might say that it grows. From his first work on hysteria Freud referred to the ego (in German simply *Ich*, the 'I') to mean something that was only a *part* of the psychic apparatus. After that it becomes a mobile and evolving concept. At times, especially in Freud's early writing, the ego seems like a person but in the later emphasis it is more like an agency. The trouble is that the idea of the ego has to do a lot of different things and no job-description fits it precisely. Leaving aside some of these theoretical complexities I shall concentrate on what the ego does.

We have already seen that the ego defends itself from certain ideas, in hysteria for example; that it is closely linked with consciousness, is opposed to the unconscious, helps to carry out the process of censorship and repression. In approaching the idea of the 'I' Freud faces a problem. His topic is the unconscious and the unconscious is basically interested in pleasure rather than reality. So when Freud wants to explain why we don't walk into lamp-posts he can't very well start with external reality as we perceive it. His solution is elegant and plausible. The ego is developed, with an awareness of reality, so that the unconscious does not waste its time pursuing objects which are imaginary and much less pleasurable than real ones:

> It was only the non-occurrence of the expected satisfaction, the disappointment experienced, that led to the abandonment of this attempt at satisfaction by means of hallucination. Instead of it, the psychical apparatus had to decide to form a conception of the real circumstances in the external world and to endeavour to make a real alteration in them.
>
> (1973–86, vol 11: 36)

Freud refers to the ego which performs this task in terms of perception and consciousness. In fact, it is here that the paths between psychology and psychoanalysis diverge, for most psychology takes the way in which individuals come to a knowledge of reality as its exclusive topic.

For the embryo in the womb there can be no distinction between itself and what's beyond it – its every need is immediately satisfied. For the newborn baby, even after the trauma of birth, most of this blissful, self-enclosed state can continue simply because babies who are not fed and cleaned by others do not survive. If you are hungry you get the breast; if you are wet and dirty you are cleaned up. Lacan jokes that the infant is an 'hommelette' (1977b: 197), spreading like egg batter on the pan, with no defined limit. At this stage the infant is neither masculine nor feminine but combines both possibilities; in French *homme* is 'man' while -*ette* is a feminine ending.

Isn't this why babies are beautiful and young children delightful? 'The charm of a child lies to a great extent in his narcissism, his self-contentment and inaccessibility', says Freud hardly pausing before he adds the usual sardonic rider, that so 'does the charm of certain animals which seem not to concern themselves about us such as cats and large beasts of prey' (1973–86, vol 11: 83).

This can't last. Gradually, often painfully, the new arrival learns it is not everything and everywhere but that it is surrounded by something else. A crawling baby bumps into things; like an impossible drunk, a toddler keeps bumping into things hard and falling over. Moving around, being weaned from the breast, having to control our urine and faeces, we quickly learn about inside and outside. The distinction gets mapped onto pleasure and unpleasure: 'A tendency arises to separate from the ego everything that can become a source of such unpleasure, to throw it outside and to create a pure pleasure-ego which is confronted by a strange and threatening "outside"' (1973–86, vol 12: 254). As a result the ego comes to detach itself from the external world: 'originally the ego includes everything, later it separates off an external world from itself' (ibid: 255).

Defence

To maintain itself the ego must not only repel real possibilities of unpleasure coming from the outside world but also defend itself against the unconscious, against drives which menace its stability by getting it too excited. As a way to cope with these threats the ego has at its disposal a wide variety of mechanisms for redirecting libido into safer channels, including repression, projection and introjection (forms of identification that will be discussed shortly), rationalisation and sublimation.

In sublimation sexual feeling is 'desexualised' by being re-directed onto non-sexual or less obviously sexual activities. Art is a very good example of sublimation. For example, instead of *actually* looking at attractive naked bodies, in most art galleries you can look at paintings of them, and even convince yourself it is educa-tional. Sublimation is particularly important in helping people to manage in social life.

Two important mechanisms of defence are denial and disavowal. The beautiful German words for these, *Verneinung* and *Verleug-nung*, fit into a series with others such as *Verdrängung* (repression) and *Verwerfung* (in Freud 'repudiation' but translated from Lacan as 'foreclosure'). These work with the German prefix, *Ver-*, suggest-ing removal and reversal, all activities of consciousness trying to hold itself together in the face of unconscious pressures. We have already come across denial in the story of the patient who tells Freud that whoever she is the person in his dream is '*not* my mother'. Another example would be Mary in Eugene O'Neill's play, *Long Day's Journey into Night*. Her son, Edmund, manifestly has tuberculosis and is racked with spasms of coughing though she keeps telling herself that it is just a cold.

Denial deals with the inner world, disavowal generally is concerned with external things. Freud's account of fetishism is an example of disavowal. He treated a young man who could not make love except to a woman with a shiny nose and concluded from his analysis that the shiny nose (and looking at it) was a fetish. The process of fetishism works like this. If a very young child imagines the mother has a penis and then comes to the con-clusion that it is missing, it can feel threatened by the idea of castration. A fetish is an object taken as a replacement for the mother's penis whose absence is thus disavowed. 'An inquisitive boy' might peer 'at the woman's genitals from below' ('Fetishism', 1973–86, vol 7: 354), and then make a fetish of something from the vicinity which he saw *before* his discovery – Freud mentions 'the foot' or 'shoe', 'fur and velvet', even 'an athletic support-belt which could also be worn as bathing drawers' (ibid: 356). That Freud has discovered something here is testified by a certain kind of pornography which specialises in fetish gear, as well as shops which sell items such as satin basques with lace trimmings, black rubber underwear, elaborate suspender belts, certain garments made of leather. By such out-of-the-way methods as fetishism the ego protects itself.

Identification

As he worked with patients Freud came across problems with the ego. Why did they consciously resist interpretations Freud had grounds for thinking were correct? How could the ego bring about repression if it were not intimately in touch with the unconscious? If someone in love gets a cold or slight toothache they quickly lose interest in the outside world and the loved one: how could this happen unless libido is being redirected from the world onto the ego itself? What is going on when you have a shower and enjoy caressing yourself all over with soapy hands? Would this not lead to direction of 'the libido to the subject's own body' (1973–86, vol 1: 465)? Recognising that the ego did not just deal with reality but was available for a variety of unconscious activities made sense of a lot of experiences people have. Identification is one such activity.

Identification is what we laugh at when a young child copies exactly and without really understanding it his mother's habit of saying, 'Well, there we are'. Identification, Lacan notes, means that 'the child who sees another fall, cries' (1977a: 19). If you are sitting on the upper deck of a bus on a pouring wet day and see a cyclist wobble uncertainly in front, you find your heart in your mouth for them, as they say – you feel you are them. Identification means that individuals brought up in a group want to become like the senior members of that group, whether that group is a nation, a clan, a football team, a family. 'The boss told me to go out and do it and I done it' the footballer who has just scored an outstanding goal says in a contented tone. The young man in the crowd at Wimbledon who (irritatingly) shouts 'Come on, Pete' to the international tennis star, Sampras, is identifying himself with someone on first name terms with the tennis star. The most far-reaching possibility of identification is that through which boys get to become like their fathers – father-figures, role-models – and girls like their mothers.

You can't identify with what you are. That is, strictly, the process of identification presupposes that subject and object – the one who does the identifying and what they identify with – remain distinct and separate. In unconscious identification they achieve resemblance through fantasy. This moves in one of two directions: either the subject goes out to the object (projection) or the subject takes the object into themselves (introjection). Identification is a form of regression because 'identification is the original form of emotional tie with an object' (1973–86, vol 12: 137), like mother and baby. An adult is always liable to return to it.

On 30 June 1998 the newspapers carried the story of a woman who was suing her employer for wrongful dismissal. In reply the company said that she had been so affected by the death of Princess Diana that she couldn't work. She spent the next week crying, talking on the phone to friends about how tragic it was and covering her desk in poems she had written for the princess. This woman didn't know Princess Di personally but, like millions of others who left flowers at Kensington Palace and wept publicly, she mourned her.

There are two questions here: why the identification? how did identification lead to mourning? Why Princess Di should be the object of such wide-spread identification is not so easy to answer because there are almost as many forms of identification as there are people who do the identifying. She was the best known young woman in the world, she was beautiful, she married a Prince, she had wealth beyond most people's wildest dreams. But she is a very open signifier. I wonder if we might explain the phenomenon along the following lines? (a) Di was very unhappy in her personal life, losing her mother at an early age, losing her husband soon after the marriage; (b) but she was in a position to compensate for this loss with a stunning exhibition of narcissism – looks, clothes, dress, style, fashionable surroundings. Is this what particularly attracts identification – that she tried specially hard to make up for rootlessness through spectacular consumption and looking good?

The Diana figure promises the pleasures not just of fantasy identification with a star ('wouldn't it be nice if I was . . .') but since 31 August 1997 with a *fallen* star. Freud marks off mourning for the dead, a largely conscious process which leads to renewal of normal life, from melancholia, an unconscious effect, in which the mourning cannot be completed, cannot be worked through. In 1861 Queen Victoria's husband, Prince Albert, died; the Queen retired from public life, wrapped herself in widow's weeds, and lived in seclusion in Windsor Castle for the next 20 years. Her mourning became melancholy, as did that of Hamlet for his father (Freud's own example). It is significant that Hamlet preserves an idealised memory of his father while referring to himself with contempt and self-hatred.

In 'Mourning and Melancholia' (1917) Freud argues that a state of melancholy expresses itself in a diminution of self-regard, 'an impoverishment' of the ego (1973–86, vol 11: 254). The ego is judged by another part of the ego, what Freud at this point calls 'the critical agency' (ibid: 256), the ego ideal, and which he later defines more precisely as the super-ego.

The lost object (Diana, Albert, old King Hamlet) can seem to be kept alive if its place is taken by the ego, if there is 'an *identification* of the ego with the abandoned object' (ibid: 258). But this only happens on condition that the ego ideal becomes active in criticising and judging the ego – the widow who endlessly reproaches herself for being responsible for her loved one's death.

A similar process may explain the pleasurably sad feeling of nostalgia, when you resuscitate an image of your former self by realising that it is gone for ever. Or the enjoyably depressing songs of the Manchester bands, with titles such as 'Girlfriend in a coma' and 'Love will tear us apart'.

THE EGO AND THE ID (1923)

Work such as this on melancholy and the two positions of identification it involves lead Freud inexorably to the conclusion that 'much of the ego is itself unconscious' (1973–86, vol 11: 290). This entails a revision in his conception of the organisation of the unconscious, usually categorised in terms of the *topographical*, the *dynamic* and the *economic*. These terms are not as formidable as they sound. Topography refers to the mapping of the system – earlier frontiers between conscious, preconscious and unconscious now give way to a division between ego, super-ego and id. The dynamic relation is that in which conscious and unconscious are actively split in the repression of the unconscious. Economy alludes to the balance and distribution of psychic energy across subjectivity.

In *The Ego and the Id* Freud recapitulates the functions of the ego:

> It is to this ego that consciousness is attached; the ego controls the approaches to motility . . . it is the mental agency which supervises all its own processes, and which goes to sleep at night, though even then it exercises the censorship in dreams. From this ego proceed the repressions . . .
>
> (1973–86, vol 11: 355)

Now he accepts that the perception–consciousness system is 'superficial' (ibid: 361) in the explicit sense that it constitutes the outer surface of the ego. The ego itself 'merges into' the id (ibid:

362). However, Freud reaffirms that the ego is a 'bodily ego' (ibid: 364) since it is the interface at which the sensations of skin, membrane and nerve in contact with the outside become psychically charged.

Building on his new understanding that, at a very deep level, identification is originally a form of 'emotional tie with an object', that desire and identification are at first very close to each other, Freud is in a position to argue that the ego develops a relation to the id. The ego – whose constant theme is deprivation and the limits to desire – can gain some control of the id by reminding it of its inevitable losses and offering itself as a substitute for them. Freud says the ego has a kind of sexual relation with the id: 'When the ego assumes the features of the object, it is forcing itself, so to speak, upon the id as a love-object and is trying to make good the id's loss by saying: "Look, you can love me too – I am so like the object"' (ibid: 369). Since the ego has no energy of its own, how otherwise can it acquire it from the id except by *seducing* it, as it were?

Identification also explains the origins of the ego ideal or super-ego when the boy tries to be like the father – like him except of course that he can't have the mother. So 'the super-ego retains the character of the father' (ibid: 374). When we were children we 'admired and feared' our parents, then later, Freud says simply, 'we took them into ourselves' (ibid: 376). The growing child begins to measure what they are against a happier memory of how they were. We idealise our earliest, narcissistic state and try 'to recover' that (1973–86, vol 11: 95), a development which reinforces our own voice of conscience.

The super-ego, this alien we have taken inside us, turns out to have some fearful properties, just as even a loving father has for a small boy such as Little Hans. Freud writes eloquently about (and, to my ear, against) the aggressiveness of the super-ego. It is exorbitant – the more you try to satisfy it by doing what it says (getting up early, going to where you should be, doing the work set, doing what you said you would do) the more it demands. It always leaves an excess of guilt sloshing around; in some circumstances it 'rages against the ego with merciless violence' (ibid: 394), becoming 'as cruel as only the id can' (ibid: 395) until it is 'a pure culture of the death instinct (drive)' (ibid: 394). In Samuel Beckett's novel, Malone feels inside him how 'the wild beast of earnestness padded up and down, roaring, ravening, rending' (1962: 25).

Daddy has two faces. The benign and all-loving Father of the Christian narrative has a place of eternal torture reserved for the ones he doesn't like. Throughout history the worst atrocities people have committed have not been from wild acts of irresponsible blood-lust but because they thought it was something they had to do; it was a *duty* to kill witches/Jews/Arabs/Africans/Christians. We may fancy that those in charge of the Nazi death-camps lived out terrible forbidden pleasures, like the masters in one of de Sade's fantasy castles. Far from it. The evidence seems to be that they performed obscene rites of sacrifice to the super-ego.

Between his arrest and execution in April 1947 Rudolf Höss, Commandant of Auschwitz, wrote an autobiography. He is lying about some things but probably not in the following, which echoes statements made by other Nazi leaders:

> As a fanatical National-Socialist I was firmly convinced that our ideals would gradually be accepted and would prevail throughout the world, after having been suitably modified in conformity with the national characteristics of the other people concerned. Jewish supremacy would thus be abolished.
>
> (1994: 55)

Höss undertakes a major role in the 'final solution to the Jewish question' as an act of supreme duty and self-discipline which he forces himself to go through with, despite feelings of horror and disgust.

Earnestness, not the lust for pleasure, is what really does the damage. In Freud's view the super-ego is the price we pay for civilisation. Sometimes it is a fearful price. He died in London in 1939, in the month the war started. If he had lived, I do not think he would have been surprised by anything that happened in the period 1939–45.

LACAN'S EGO

Effectively, Freud offers two somewhat disjunct theories of the ego. According to one its main function is dealing with reality through perception and consciousness; according to another it is structured in relation to unconscious desire – 'Look, you can love me too'. Lacan's conception of the ego and identity follows very much Freud's second line of analysis. I think it will be helpful, therefore, to cite a passage in which Lacan makes it clear that he believes nevertheless that we do indeed perceive a real world though it is always taken up in terms of fantasy and desire:

> The theoretical difficulties encountered by Freud seem to me in fact to derive from the mirage of objectification, inherited from classical psychology, constituted by the idea of the *perception/consciousness* system, in which Freud seems suddenly to fail to recognise the existence of everything that the ego neglects, scotomises, misconstrues in the sensations that make it react to reality, everything that it ignores, exhausts, and binds in the significations that it receives from language . . .
>
> (1977a: 22)

(Scotomisation is when an image isn't seen because it falls on the blind spot in the retina.)

Everybody sees the same world but from the whole field of vision everybody notices different things. I am particularly good at finding things which have got lost, I suspect because I hate losing them. In an argument between sexual partners a banal fact, such as who forgot to get the milk, can get tangled up in complicated strands of interpretation so that a whole relationship can turn on a triviality: 'it shows you don't love me'.

Reality is there, no doubt about it, but we each experience it for ourselves. Is it only reality and reason which determine the decisions we make? Why, for example, do people choose the jobs they do? Why become a surgeon, who cuts up people's bodies, rather than a computer programmer? Or a dentist, who has to hurt people's mouths (do they unconsciously want to)? Why does someone else enjoy handling and selling fruit ('all nice and juicy') while another mends sewers? The ego and its choices have a rational component but are not just rational.

The mirror stage

Each of us arrives into human culture from the outside, though we come equipped with a genetic programme that allows us to learn any human language there is. How is it that within five or six years the newly arrived little animal you bring home with you from the hospital has become a person, who speaks your language, shares your assumptions, can go off to school and answer its own name when the teacher calls it out? Why do people born in England generally grow up to be English rather than Nepalese? And what does it mean for an individual to 'be' anything?

Lacan's answer is that identity is a form of *identification*, that the subject's ego is 'that which is reflected of his form in his objects' (1977a: 194) ('subject' has to be 'he' and 'his' because it translates the French '*le* sujet'). Identity is borrowed from what Lacan names as 'the Other'. The Other consists of law, society and other people; but since I can only relate to these on the shared basis of the signifier, the Other is encountered as 'the symbolic order', the organisation of signifiers that surround me. Since my identity is not *really* me but an identity internalised from the symbolic order and treated as me, Lacan subscribes to Arthur Rimbaud's statement that 'I is an other' (ibid: 23).

In his essay on 'The Mirror Stage' Lacan does refer to literal looking in literal mirrors but is explicit that this *exemplifies* the construction of identity because the mirror which matters to us is *other people* (see ibid: 1–7). We might think of a baby surrounded by loving adults – 'Who's a gorgeous little thing, then?', and who becomes what they treat it as. Here it is worth keeping in mind that for Lacan people need language not to transmit messages, to *say* something to someone, but in the first place because they want to *be* someone for somebody. The mirror stage, however, predates language.

A toddler between the ages of six and 18 months responds to its mirror image 'with a flutter of jubilant activity' (ibid: 1) while other animals treat it with indifference or as a competitor. What the young child experiences in a mirror is a unified image of its own body, a *Gestalt* or organised pattern. This contrasts strongly with its own sense of its own body, definitely not in its control, 'sunk', says Lacan, 'in motor incapacity and nursling dependence' (ibid: 2). It must seem to a small child that its various bits – feet, knees, hands, elbows, head – have a will of their own and keep painfully running into things. In comparison with the permanence and unity of its own mirror image the child feels its body as 'fragmented' (ibid: 4). This is Lacan's famous idea of the 'body in pieces' or *corps morcelé*.

Dry-mouthed terror at the possibility of your body coming to bits is fundamental to human experience. It is Lacan's version of 'the worst thing in the world . . . images of castration, mutilation, dismemberment, dislocation, evisceration, devouring, bursting open of the body' (ibid: 11). Surely this is a dazzling insight? If as Freud argues the fear of death is only the anticipated shadow of castration, then death for each of us, we know, can only happen if the body first comes to pieces. Unless the image of dismemberment were hugely charged for us, how could you explain why we are, alas, the only species which enjoys deliberately taking to pieces members of its own kind?

Faced with either imaginary unity in the mirror image or the body in pieces the young subject is catapulted away from fragmentation into identification with its mirror image, what Lacan calls the 'ideal I' – apparently stable, perfect and unified, in control of its parts. This is the 'I' in a primordial form before it enters language and before it becomes a speaking subject whose ego is supported by internalising signifiers from the symbolic order. Even then, just as much as in the earlier mirror stage, identity is *acquired* from the Other, a form of fantasy and misrecognition.

The mirror stage 'situates the agency of the ego, before its social determination, in a fictional direction' (ibid: 2). The bad news and the good news are the same – there's no real me and this identity I think is me is the best I'll ever have. My ego seems to be the same in space, permanent across time and unified in substance, though in all of these I misrecognise how I come about as an *effect*, thinking I'm really there, despite different spaces, times, my own actual dispersal into various selves, being split between conscious and unconscious.

Hollywood from way back has mounted a good line of impassive, rock-like heroes such as John Wayne and Clint Eastwood. Recently that idea has come to be represented by the cyborg, such as the one in *RoboCop* (1987) or the replicants of *Blade Runner* (1982). *Terminator 2* (1991) has two cyborgs, one good (Arnold Schwarzenegger), one bad. Through its unbelievable capacity to survive, the cyborg represents the permanence of the ego. In *Terminator 2* the cyborgs pass through fire, fall from a height, get thrown from a fast car, walk through walls, are gassed, pierced with iron bars, blown up, and shot endlessly. All with impunity (damaged they repair themselves). At one point the bad one walks into a cloud of liquid nitrogen until he freezes solid and his feet break off. Hit with bullets, his body then explodes into a thousand pieces. These fall to the floor where they are melted by the heat of a nearby furnace. Drops run together and coagulate like mercury until from the silver pool a phallic figure rises, spectacularly reconstituted.

What gives away the fact that the cyborg attracts the same identification as the bodily image in the mirror stage is not its physical unity, control and mastery. The point is cyborgs have no feelings. The ego is threatened by all forms of drive but not the cyborg because it has no unconscious and no desire. Identification? Anyone who has taken a crew of eight-year-olds to *Terminator 2* for a birthday treat will know that for weeks after the order 'clean your teeth' will be answered with 'No problemo'. The adult ego, which seems so absolutely sure of itself, comes about by impersonating early models until the mask becomes a face (almost).

The idealised I and the I idealised

Lacan marks off the ideal ego from the ego ideal (see 1988a: 141), a distinction which arises from two contrasted modes of identification (and his concept of the ego ideal is not the same as Freud's). For Lacan the ideal ego is defined in the way the subject projects itself onto objects, moves out into identification with them. The ego ideal, on the other hand, develops when external objects are taken in or introjected. The subject's ideal ego appears at 'that point at which he desires to gratify himself in himself' (Lacan 1977b: 257), the ego ideal at 'the point . . . from which the subject will see himself, as one says, *as others see him*' (ibid: 268). A person's ego ideal is being challenged when someone asks, 'Who does he think he is?' or 'Who does she think she is?'.

In the story of Narcissus in Ovid the youth at first loves his own image in the water, projecting himself onto it, but later, realising that he is this image, takes it in as a version of himself. The ideal ego develops in the mirror stage, in what Lacan calls 'the imaginary'; it emerges as the ego ideal with language, in the symbolic, when the child learns to confirm its identity, for example, by answering to its name. Both transformations of the ego are idealised, me as I'd like to see myself. And both – the whole ego in fact – is for Lacan a source of delusion, leading us to believe in our own fantasies, our own importance, our imagined control of the world around us.

Everybody, to a greater or lesser extent, trusts in and lives out their own ego ideal. If we were to cast this in moralising terms, then we might think of it simply as hypocrisy or self-deception. A group of (generally) middle-aged men sit at a meeting discussing the 'mission statement' of their project, how 'empowerment' will substantiate 'individual profiles' in the search for 'excellence' and 'quality enhancement' without for one minute realising how vacuous their whole discourse is. A woman congratulates herself because she is such a dedicated teacher and spends so much time helping students – she is in fact a dull teacher and messes up the students she counsels. Each of Jane Austen's novels contains one hopelessly indulgent and adoring mother who lets her children behave appallingly. And, no doubt, people who write books about the unconscious are sure they know enough to tell other people all about it.

It is fatally easy to see how the ego ideal affects other people, but seeing it in oneself is blocked by repression. The ego ideal deceives us *especially* when we think we have got the better of it – 'I know I'm absolutely objective and fair-minded' and 'I can see my own faults but don't give in to them' and 'Though I was tempted to appoint X because she's a friend, in fact she is the best person for the job'. Lacan is merciless, referring us to 'the mirage that renders modern man so sure of being himself even in his uncertainties about himself, and even in the mistrust he has learned to practise against the traps of self-love' (1977a: 165).

Merciless to others but not to himself: his biographer remarks that Lacan 'often described to his patients and pupils the dangers of believing in the omnipotence of the ego, but it never occurred to him to apply this wisdom to himself' (Roudinesco 1997: 247–48).

It is well known that prisons contain only people who have been wrongfully imprisoned after a miscarriage of justice – this is the work of the ego ideal, which also seems to dictate that people who have committed atrocities cannot admit it. Recently, in South Africa, the Truth and Reconciliation Commission, which has been trying to establish the facts of what went on under Apartheid, took evidence from a group of very able scientists and medical men who had worked for the previous regime in a biological warfare unit. On 14 July 1998 some of this footage was shown on British television, and reported the next day:

> Neils Knobel, a former South African surgeon-general, explained without any hint of a guilty conscience, how South Africa had acquired biological warfare secrets from the UK, the USA and USSR. He admitted that he'd experimented with bacterial agents to cause infertility among the black population.
>
> (*Guardian*, 15 July 1998)

The unit also considered ways to put cholera in the water supply of black neighbourhoods and how to breed a version of anthrax immune to penicillin. 'Without any hint of a guilty conscience': you can pull a story like that from the newspapers every month.

The ego ideal leads us to collaborate with the fantasy that people are fundamentally good-hearted and do the best they can in a world which is bright, transparent, harmonious and getting better, a utopian vision endlessly repeated to us by the media. People cling to what they like to think others think of them.

There is a broad contrast here between Freud and Lacan. While Freud takes the view that unhappiness is caused essentially by repression, Lacan believes the damage is caused by the power with which we live out the ego ideal. You have to have an identity, of course, there's no escape from that. But for Lacan it is better if you can accept your fantasies as fantasies and not as the real thing, ways of representing yourself, not life itself. He writes of being the dummy hand at bridge, the one whose cards are all laid face up on the table – you just sit there while the others play them for you. But they're still your cards and it's still you they're being played for.

Or, to return to the example of *Hamlet*. Throughout most of the play Hamlet has been wholly embroiled in fantasy – mourning his father, hating his mother, expressing horror and contempt for Ophelia. Lacan singles out the moment after Hamlet has come back from his sea-voyage, with a new sense of irony and self-detachment and proceeds to carry out his mission. Laertes, says Lacan, is Hamlet's ego ideal, full of his certainty and self-importance, Hamlet's double whom he must kill. At the end Laertes challenges Hamlet to a duel, but the fight is fixed:

> Hamlet responds to this necessity only on a disinterested level, that of the tournament. He commits himself in what we might call a formal, or even a fictive way. He is, in truth, entering the most serious of games, without knowing it. In that game he will lose his life – in spite of himself. He is going out – again, without knowing it – to meet his act and his death, which, but for an interval of a few moments, will coincide.
>
> Everything that he saw in the aggressive relationship was only a sham, a mirage. What does that mean? It means that he has entered into the game without, shall we say, his phallus . . . He does enter into the game, nevertheless.
>
> (1977c: 32)

Hamlet has learned to become, as Lacan says, a 'foil' to Laertes but not a sword – there but not *really* there. Sanity does not mean trying to be yourself but accepting instead that you can only be for others.

BEING IN LOVE

The psychoanalytic account of love forms a bridge between this section, on narcissism, and the next, on sexuality. Most people would think of love, dyadic love between the sexes, or in a same-sex relationship, as sexual. Both Freud and Lacan regard being in love as an expression of narcissism, not love for the other but self-love, self-deception. Lacan said he loved his dog, Justine, because 'she never mistakes me for anyone else' (cited in Hill 1997: 77).

Freud discusses being in love in relation to melancholy. In melancholy the lost object is put in the place of the ego and the ego ideal is active in judging the ego. In love, by contrast, the object becomes identified with the ego ideal. Being in love happens if a loved one, rather than being lost, simply cannot be obtained and desire satisfied. The unattainable object can seem to be possessed, however, if it is '*put in the place of the ego ideal*' (*Group Psychology and the Analysis of the Ego*, 1973–86, vol 12: 144). In consequence, the ego becomes impoverished:

> The impulsions whose trend is towards directly sexual satisfaction may now be pushed into the background entirely, as regularly happens, for instance, with a young man's sentimental passion; the ego becomes more and more unassuming and modest, and the object more and more sublime and precious, until at last it gets possession of the entire self-love of the ego, whose self-sacrifice thus follows as a natural consequence.
>
> (ibid: 143)

The lover who overvalues someone like this shows 'traits of humility', even of 'self-injury' (ibid.). Because it has been set up in the ego ideal 'everything the object does and asks for is right and blameless' (ibid: 144). In the film of *The English Patient*, set in North Africa in the early years of the Second World War, a Hungarian Count and a married woman, Catherine Clifton, fall desperately in love. When she dies, the Count betrays all his allegiances and friends by giving some crucial maps to the German enemy in exchange for a plane to fly Catherine's body out of the desert: she is now all that matters to him.

For Lacan to love is 'essentially, to wish to be loved' (1977b: 253). It is not something you can do for yourself because it depends on another to see you as you would like to be seen – or rather, imagining such an other. The romantic love tradition claims that each sees and responds to the other in a perfectly *reciprocal* relation. In 'The Good-Morrow' John Donne writes, 'My face in thine eye, thine in mine appears', using the fact that an eye viewed close-up reflects the face of the viewer to suggest a completely mutual and requited love. But the metaphor is a deception because me seeing you can never coincide with you seeing me. As Lacan puts it, 'When, in love, I solicit a look, what is profoundly unsatisfying and always missing is that – *You never look at me from the place from which I see you*' (ibid: 103).

This disjunction (me seeing you/you seeing me) is brought about by the Other, the symbolic order in which other subjects are situated behind or within the signifiers which relate in the first place to each other ('a signifier . . . represents a subject not for another subject but for another signifier'). But the Other can be *imagined* as a point from which someone looks at you: 'Love is essentially deception', says Lacan, introducing 'a perspective centred on the Ideal point, capital I, placed somewhere in the Other, from which the Other sees me, in the form I like to be seen' (1977b: 268). This needs a little unpacking.

For Lacan, love involves a series of fantasy identifications in which the object is taken up into the self. First, the Other as a whole is misrecognised and appropriated as a single point. This is further misrecognised as the *eyes* of the beloved. These are treated like a mirror in the mirror stage, reflecting the lover in a more perfect form. But the eyes are imagined not as a passive mirror but as a person with an adoring gaze wholly occupied in looking at the viewer. In this look the lover is seen not as they are but as they want to imagine themselves to be: the perfect lover, the ideal self. Being in love, says Lacan forcefully, has therefore a 'fundamentally narcissistic structure' (ibid: 186). When Humphrey Bogart says, 'Here's looking at you, kid', he really means, 'Look at me as I want to be looked at'.

The absence of the sexual relation

There is, Lacan concludes, 'no sexual relation' (1982: 143), sexual relation, that is, not as intercourse but as a mutually satisfying *rapport* such that each reflects the other, each feels 'You are everything and everything is you'. Love is impossible because love is a disguised form of self-love: 'when one is a man, one sees in one's partner what can serve, narcissistically, to act as one's own support' (ibid: 157). When one is a woman, likewise. Love is impossible because, as far as Lacan is concerned, the sexes are completely asymmetrical in their desires, something we shall discuss in more detail later.

When Tristan and Iseult are found together in the woods they have a sword laid between them; Denis de Rougemont (1956) argues that in the courtly love tradition love is imagined as an impossible transcendence which can only be maintained if sexual feeling is not fulfilled. And that tradition continues into Romantic love where the stories everyone remembers are those in which love is tragically *not* fulfilled because something prevents it (the warring families in *Romeo and Juliet*, unhappy marriage in *Anna Karenina*, age difference in *Lolita*). Lacan says this 'is an altogether refined way of making up for the absence of sexual relation by pretending that it is we who put an obstacle to it' (ibid: 141).

What is masked by the obstacle is the absence itself. Rob Lapsley and Michael Westlake have extended the analysis in a brilliant essay on contemporary cinema (1993): 'Jack Nicholson and Susan Sarandon romping together amidst pink balloons [in

The Witches of Eastwick (1987)], or Jonathan Switcher [Andrew McCarthy] in *Mannequin* (1987) kissing his "living doll" atop a mound of teddy bears, are less than utterly convincing as representations of sexual rapport' (ibid: 193).

In fact, Hollywood has developed three narrative structures to suggest the presence of the sexual relation while masking its actual absence: it will take place after the story ends (*Pretty Woman* and hundreds of other films); it was really there before the story begins (the lost idyll in Paris in *Casablanca* (1942)); it would take place 'if only'. 'If only' is a very rich strategy, which includes: if only she hadn't died (*Love Story* (1970) and many, many more); if only there hadn't been a Russian Revolution (*Dr Zhivago* (1965)); if only he'd had normal fingers (*Edward Scissorhands* (1990)); if only the ship hadn't hit an iceberg (*Titanic* (1997)).

From this somewhat disabused analysis of love we can turn to what psychoanalysis actually has to say about sexuality.

4

THE UNCONSCIOUS AND SEXUALITY

What we describe as our 'character' is based on the memory-traces of our impressions; and, moreover, the impressions which have had the greatest effect on us – those of our earliest youth.

(Freud 1973–86, vol 4: 689)

For most of the history of Christendom small children were considered to be dirty, demanding animals, who suddenly, when they began to talk sensibly, turned into small, incompetent adults. It is hard to exaggerate the severity handed out to children; babies were sent to wet-nurses if their parents were rich and to anyone who would feed them if they were poor. Regarded as irrational and unregenerate children were beaten without mercy.

If that attitude has now changed in the West, it is largely due to one man, Benjamin Spock. His book, *Baby and Child Care*, published in 1946, with tact, modesty and supreme authority, told parents that what young children needed above all was love, from start to finish. Spock derived this idea from Freud.

The most popular subject in Italian Renaissance painting is not the Crucifixion or the Resurrection – it is the Madonna and Child. When he was trying to discern what in our earliest experiences was so determining for later life Freud came to the same insight as Giotto, Cimabue, Fra Angelico, Masaccio, Bellini and many others: 'No one who has seen a baby sinking back satiated from the breast and falling asleep with flushed cheeks and a blissful smile can escape the reflection that this picture persists as a prototype of the expression of sexual satisfaction in later life' (1973–86, vol 7: 98). It is possible that this is the reason the language of sexual intimacy so often takes the form of baby talk. And it is certainly not surprising that in battle, wounded soldiers, brave or not, cry for their mothers.

One reason why the human infant is thrown so violently into that early dyadic relation, a reason put forward by both Freud and Lacan, is that we are born too soon. To get our huge heads past the pelvis and out into the world we arrive earlier and less developed than other mammals. Unlike a baby kangaroo we have no pouch to go to, and therefore we *have* to be carefully looked after for a long time.

That transition we make from birth to five years (say), from animal into a speaking subject, has a conclusive effect, though the consequences may be very good or very bad. We all know that young children who are loved and looked after come to love themselves and others, while children who are ignored and ill-treated grow up hating themselves and the world – the abused become abusers. In *Seminar 1* Lacan records the terrible story of Robert (1988a: 91–106). I do not know of anything in literature as harrowing as these documentary pages.

Robert was abandoned by his father, from birth hated and neglected by his mother; by three years and nine months he had had 25 changes of residence. He was hyperactive, a prey to jerky and disorderly movements, as well as convulsive fits of agitation, and would accompany even the simplest moments of routine with 'piercing howls'; he was constantly violent towards others and himself. All he can say are the two words, '*Miss!*' and '*wolf*!'. On one occasion he threw food, plates and everything across the dining-hall; and one evening, 'while standing on his bed in front of the other terrified children', he tried to cut off his penis with a pair of scissors.

Robert made his helper 'play the role' of the mother who starved him, forcing her to sit on a chair so that she would knock over a mug of milk, which caused him to howl. Deprived of a coherent image of himself from others, he was 'acutely confused as to his own self, the contents of his body, objects, children, and the adults who surrounded him'. Treated as a detested and predatory outcast, he became that creature: seeing his reflection in the glass of a window 'he hit it, crying out – *Wolf! Wolf!*'.

ORAL AND ANAL

Drive is 'a concept on the frontier between the mental and the somatic' (1973–86, vol 11: 118). When neurologists diagram the body in terms of our sensitivity to it – the so-called 'motor cortex homunculus' – the mouth and genitals are enormous (for some reason a veil seems to be drawn over the backside). The body and its points of pleasure, its orifices and exciting surfaces, shape the subject's developing experience. Freud distinguishes three of these zones. Not surprisingly, the first is oral pleasure, pleasures of the mouth as felt by the infant at the breast, sucking and thumb-sucking. A small child is so preoccupied by sucking it will try to put almost anything in its mouth. With weaning the breast is lost, and there follows an endless chain of substitutions which begins with sweets, ice lollies, chewing gum, progresses to all kinds of food and drink, and then on to other substitutes such as cigarettes, kissing, gin and tonic, Stilton cheese, Château-Neuf du Pape. Everyone will have their own personal list. Sadly, for reasons we will come to, though each of these tries to recover the actual pleasure of the breast, none of them matches the immediate and unthinking ecstasy of the infant.

As well as the mouth, pleasure also comes from the anus and urethra, which is associated with all that passes that way. Those who find this implausible have not spent enough time with young children. I have known respectable households which have spent weeks obsessed with nothing else but whether their child can or cannot solve the riddle of its sphincter. Or try telling a six-year-old you want to whisper a joke and when you've got their attention, just say 'Poo! Poo!'. It won't always work but in the right circumstances you will be rewarded with fits of giggles. Or listen to what comedians actually say, because much of the time they tell 'shit' jokes or even 'eat-shit' jokes. I heard once a story on late-night television too gross to put in cold print except to say it involves a waiter reproached for having his thumb in the soup and his explanation of how he usually kept his thumb warm.

Unless house-trained, animals shit and piss whenever they feel like it whereas people have to learn to hold back. 'It is here [i.e in toilet-training] for the first time', writes Freud, 'that they encounter the external world as an inhibiting power, hostile to their desire for pleasure' (1973–86, vol 1: 357). Shit is polysemous. To the infant its faeces seem to be a part of its own body it does not want to lose, along with the pleasure it gives, so it may try to hold onto them. Shit is also a gift, the first thing the child produces all on its own ('do it for mummy'); release signals compliance while withholding suggests disobedience.

Shit symbolises money for us, as Freud points out (in 'Character and Anal Eroticism', 1973–86, vol 7: 209–15). We call it 'filthy lucre', we say someone has a 'pile' of it, is 'stinking rich', or 'rolling in it'. 'Dirt is matter in the wrong place', says Freud (ibid: 213): keeping things clean and tidy is a way of ensuring that you are a million miles away from the practices of some naughty children Freud refers to who do 'all sorts of unseemly things with the faeces that had been passed' (ibid: 210).

In another essay, whose mildly academic title, 'On Transformation of Instinct as Exemplified by Anal Eroticism', belies its controversial and indeed lurid content, Freud argues that for everyone at a deep level there is a series which he diagrams as: '*faeces* (money, gift), *baby, penis*' (1973–86, vol 7: 296). Faeces equating to money and gift we have encountered already. For the others Freud suggests that they take on a symbolic equivalence because 'Faeces, penis and baby are all three solid bodies; they all three, by forcible entry or expulsion, stimulate a membraneous passage, i.e. the rectum and the vagina, the latter being as it were "taken on lease" from the rectum' (ibid: 302). Some years ago there was a television advertisement for chocolates in which a handsome man landed from a helicopter, sneaked into a woman's room and left beside her bed a box full of these intensely pleasurable, small, elongated black objects. Could they signify faeces/money/gift/penis/baby?

ORAL, ANAL – AND GENITAL

Genital is where the fun really begins, though it would be a mistake to think that oral, anal and genital are neat phases you pass through in that order and somehow emerge on the other side. The unconscious pleasures associated with these phases are all caught up together and stay with us throughout life. For both little boys and little girls the erogenous attractions of the genitals begin soon after birth.

Freud shocked the late Victorian world by affirming that sexuality begins in infancy though this should not have been a surprise for parents. It is not unusual to put the bed covers back over a young child and find it with one hand firmly stuck in its mouth and the other in its groin. Freud asserts that thumb-sucking in early infancy may be 'combined with rubbing some sensitive part of the body such as the breast or the external genitalia' and that a path leads from 'sucking to masturbation' (1973–86, vol 7: 96). At four years old Little Hans was very frankly interested in sex. So anxious are we to protect our children from any premature awareness of sexuality that the Barbie doll has no nipples and Action Man no genitals.

Oral, anal, genital or any mixture of the three: young children can disturb us with what they get up to without compunction, and this includes doing 'unseemly things with the faeces'. As Freud points out, however, this relatively unrepressed state is subject to childhood amnesia. It is a remarkable fact that you can have a fairly coherent conversation with a child as young as four but that none of us have any but the most shadowy memories of ourselves before ten. The reason is simple: these earliest impressions get repressed.

In the early days everyone, says Freud, has a potential to be 'polymorphously perverse' (ibid: 109). By passing into (and hopefully out of) the Oedipus complex, this bundle of polymorphous unconscious pleasures gets organised around single gender identities. It is supposed to work like this:

- the little boy seeks the mother in terms of active genital pleasure;
- he is threatened with castration;
- fear of castration and the incestuous feeling are repressed;
- the boy redirects his desire from the mother to another adult woman;
- he identifies with the father.

This progression explains the evolution of masculine identity but it leaves unresolved the question of feminine identity. Freud began by assuming that for little girls the logic was simply reversed:

- the little girl seeks the father;
- she is threatened with castration;
- castration and incestuous feeling are repressed;
- she redirects desire to another adult man;
- and identifies with the mother.

Even in his early writing this is far from certain and Freud gives a number of reasons why. In comparison with the analysis of men that of women is 'veiled' (ibid: 63); there is 'the stunting effect of civilized conditions' (ibid.); their key experiences occur in their 'first attachment to the mother' and this, being so early, is 'difficult to grasp in analysis' (ibid: 373). By 1931 and the essay on 'Female Sexuality' he says he has 'long given up any expectation of a neat parallelism between male and female sexual development' (ibid: 372).

The second problem is that in practice Oedipus just never works out. The first object, for little girls and little boys, is the mother:

> From this time onwards, the human individual has to devote himself to the great task of detaching himself [sic] from his parents . . . For the son this task consists in detaching his libidinal wishes from his mother and employing them for the choice of a real outside love-object, and in reconciling himself with his father if he has remained in opposition to him, or in freeing himself from his pressure if, as a reaction to infantile rebelliousness he has become subservient to him. These tasks are set to everyone.
>
> (1973–86, vol 1: 380)

Then Freud concludes: 'it is remarkable how seldom they are dealt with in an ideal manner'. In fact 'normal performance of the sexual function' is the result 'of a very complicated process' (1973–86, vol 10: 238).

MASCULINITY

Bob Geldof's mother died when he was quite young. In his autobiography, *Is That It?* (1986), he recalls his mother as a kind of Virgin Mary, a 'pale figure . . . standing at the top of the stairs smiling down at me' (ibid: 35). Soon after his mother's death he embezzled his dinner money and was severely beaten by his father. 'From that day on,' he says, 'my father and I were at loggerheads' (ibid: 27). This is one version of the son whose Oedipal task will consist of 'reconciling himself with his father'. Here, somewhat speculatively, is another.

On the 30 June 1998, in England's key match with Argentina in the World Cup, David Beckham retaliated against Diego Simeone of Argentina, got sent off and (supposedly) lost England the game. Beckham is not generally a dirty player so why did he do it? Could it be that his aggression against Simeone was displaced from Glenn Hoddle, the then English manager and pompous father-figure, who had refused to select Beckham for the first two matches?

In our culture the rebellious son seems more apparent than the one who 'has become subservient' to his father and must therefore free himself from him. The great archetype, no doubt, would be Jesus, the son who dies in absolute submission to the father ('not my will, but thine, be done') and never wins through to get another adult woman for himself.

Structure

In whatever balance of rebellion and compliance, the Oedipal series for masculinity can be simplified into *two* moves:

little boy → mother → other adult woman

Far from masculinity being transparent, solid and straightforward, as one might suppose, Freud's view is that it is fragile and uncertain, though generally in denial (*Verneinung*) of its own weakness.

Tendencies

Male-dominated society has traditionally promoted an opposition between Sacred and Profane Love and accordingly classified women as ideal or disparaged. The effects of this 'Double Image' are well known and it is not possible to move around in Western culture without tripping over it. It is perfectly, if harshly, expressed by what a man says, quoting 'an old Italian saying' in Truffaut's film *The Bride Wore Black* (1967), 'All women are whores except my mother who is a saint'.

In the second of his 'Contributions to the Psychology of Love' Freud offers an explanation of why men impose a false and oppressive 'Double Image' on women. He begins by claiming that all men suffer to some extent from 'psychical impotence' (1973–86, vol 7: 248). In their early years boys experience an affectionate feeling directed at the mother, who is overvalued. At puberty this is supplemented with a sensual current directed at another adult woman, who is depreciated by contrast. Masculinity faces the task of separating the two images, so that a man desires only sexual objects 'which do not recall the incestuous figures forbidden to it' (ibid: 251). Freud generalises ruefully about men, 'Where they love they do not desire and where they desire they cannot love' (ibid.). What makes the development of masculine sexuality so tricky is that it has to deal with two objects, the mother and the other adult woman, and these touch directly onto each other. As we shall see, that is not the situation for women.

Recently Linda Grant, a women's columnist, was wondering publicly 'why are men like that?' (*Guardian*, 21 July 1998), specifically complaining about why men run off and leave women who love them. She just could not understand why. Yet Freud offers an explanation in this second 'Contribution' with its gloomy account of why men can love or desire but are not good at doing both.

Relation to Super-ego

The logic of the Oedipus complex is that incestuous wishes are immediately answered by the threat of castration. In 'Dissolution of the Oedipus Complex' (1924) Freud asserts that what destroys 'the child's phallic genital organisation' is 'this threat of castration' (1973–86, vol 7: 317). However, the child's own narcissism turns it away from Oedipus and castration, in a move which replaces desire for an object with identification. For these reasons, 'the authority of the father or the parents is introjected into the ego' (ibid: 319), that is, taken from outside and internalised. This works particularly well for the little boy because the threat of castration comes to him strongly and because, in identifying with the father, he is identifying with the same sex. In fact, so optimistic does Freud feel about how well this process works for little boys that in a paper written in the following year he claims that 'in ideal cases, the Oedipus complex exists no longer, even in the unconscious'. The 'super-ego has become its heir' (ibid: 341).

FEMININITY

At the end of his essay on the 'Dissolution of the Oedipus Complex' Freud speculates about the female super-ego and then concludes that his insight into the processes in girls is 'unsatisfactory, incomplete and vague' (1973–86, vol 7: 321). Ernest Jones in his biography reported that 'Freud found the psychology of women more enigmatic than that of men' and once said to Marie Bonaparte that he had not been able after thirty years to answer the question, 'What does a woman want?' (1956, 2: 468, cited in 1973–86, vol 7: 326, fn.).

At this point two responses are likely. It could be said simply that Freud was a man and therefore could not possibly understand women; this would ignore the fact that there have been a number of female analysts who do not seem to have done much better. Or we could recognise the problems faced by a theory of the unconscious in approaching subjects whose lives have been obscured by patriarchy, and agree with Juliet Mitchell in her groundbreaking work, *Psychoanalysis and Feminism*, when she points out that 'psychoanalysis is not a recommendation *for* a patriarchal society *but* an analysis of one' (1975: xv).

Structure

If we construct a diagram of the masculine Oedipal transition in the following way:

little boy → mother → other adult woman

then the feminine equivalent would show that it actually isn't equivalent at all:

little girl → mother → father → other adult man.

The little girl also takes the mother as her first object but then faces the task of redirecting her desire (if she does) from one sex to the other, a process which involves *three* terms, not just two.

It is arguable that for a woman the mother does not fall under the same shadow of the prohibition on incest as she does for the male and so remains more easily available. An example may be the possible asymmetry between men and women in their relation to the oral, the breast and the mother. A few years ago a picture of a pleasant middle-aged lady in an attractive middle-aged hat was used to advertise the oozing seductions of chocolate eclairs with the slogan 'naughty but nice', a phrase combining oral pleasure with a hint of sexual desire. Would it be possible to sell beer to men with the slogan 'naughty but nice'? Or is it rather the case that every last trace of sexuality has to be carefully excluded from such advertisements?

Tendencies

'What does a woman want?': in Freud's view both the little boy and the little girl begin in the same way, actively directing phallic desire at the mother. This, he argued, is part of the way that *all* children attribute to everyone, '*including females, the possession of a penis*' (1973–86, vol 7: 193). A girl's clitoris 'behaves just like a penis to begin with' (ibid: 320) until she compares it with a boy's penis and realises that she 'has "come off badly"' (ibid.). The girl therefore experiences castration 'as an accomplished fact' while to the little boy it merely comes as a threat (ibid: 321)

She slips 'from the penis to a baby' (ibid.), a wish that inaugurates the Oedipus complex leading her to take 'her father as a love-object' (ibid: 340); encountering her mother's jealousy, her desire moves to another adult man. Here she becomes liable to a lesser and different version of the Double Image for the other adult man will always be a disappointment: he is 'never the right man' since typically it is the father 'who has first claims to a woman's love' (ibid: 277).

All of this is by way of a preliminary explanation. Two late essays, 'Female Sexuality' (1931; see 1973–86, vol 7: 371–92) and 'Femininity' (1933), written when Freud was in his late seventies and testosterone had ceased to exert much influence on the author's constitution, revise the previous analysis. He still maintains that castration comes to the girl as something already carried out but attributes this now not to a merely anatomical fact (clitoris versus penis) but *to the mother*, for the little girl reproaches her mother for not giving her 'a proper penis' (ibid: 381). Castration is discovered in the site of the mother's body. According to Freud's own revision of his earlier argument this view enables Juliet Mitchell to suggest that this is exactly what one would expect in a patriarchal and phallocentric culture.

From this point three pathways diverge: 1) The little girl can simply give up sexuality altogether; 2) She can disavow her loss, clinging 'with defiant self-assertiveness to her threatened masculinity', hoping to get 'a penis some time' (ibid: 376); (Freud acknowledges the reality of trajectory (2) though it is his view that this 'masculine complex' can lead to all kinds of terrible things

– female homosexuality, even feminism); 3) this trajectory follows exactly the line Freud first thought was normal for all women, that is, passing from the mother to the father and so to another adult man. Even so, he concedes, the path along which feminine sexuality develops is 'very circuitous' (ibid.).

Circuitous or not, trajectory (3) is not hard to illustrate. In the 1942 Hollywood romance, *Now, Voyager*, Charlotte (Bette Davis) is the adult daughter of a strict and oppressive widowed mother. Her mother has totally undermined her self-belief, referring to her – to her face – as 'my ugly duckling', saying contemptuously that she has 'more illnesses than a mouldy canary'. Charlotte has become silent and nervy, wears dowdy clothes, clumpy shoes, has bushy eyebrows and crimped, untidy hair. An older man, Dr Jakwith (Claude Rains), is brought to see Charlotte and wins her confidence; he accuses the mother of trying 'to destroy your daughter's life', persuades Charlotte to come to his rest home and encourages her to go on a cruise.

On this cruise she meets another man, who is older and married; a veil is drawn over whether the relationship is ever consummated. Charlotte returns home a different woman, confident, stylish, a hostess. He will not leave his sickly wife but they will continue to see each other. Charlotte is given control over his daughter ('our child', he says). The film ends with them smoking cigarettes together and Bette Davis speaking the immortal line, 'Don't let's ask for the moon – we have the stars'.

Relation to super-ego

Freud's later theory of femininity does not require him to rethink his earlier account of the difficulties women have in acceding to the super-ego. So far I have not stressed Freud's distinction between the castration complex and the Oedipus complex, a distinction clarified as Freud's work develops. While the castration complex arises from a perceived difference *between* the sexes, the

Oedipus complex is formed around desire for the parent of the opposite sex linked to rivalry with the one of the same sex. Because, according to Freud, the penis is visible and present, castration weighs unevenly on the two sexes – a *threat* to little boys, 'an accomplished fact' for little girls (1973–86, vol 7: 321) (Juliet Mitchell argues that perception of this 'fact' derives from patriarchy rather than anatomy).

In boys, desire for the mother continues to activate this threat of castration, pushing them into identification with the father, and (hopefully) the dissolution of their Oedipus complex. In girls, if castration is *already* a fact, it is not so readily available as a continuing factor in their conflict with the mother for the father. For this reason Freud does not believe women can enter into such a strong identification with the father and, therefore, their super-ego is 'never so inexorable, so impersonal, so independent of its emotional origins as we require it to be in men' (ibid: 342).

Although this whole book necessarily takes the form of an interpretation, a reading, I have set myself the limitation of not offering a critical commentary. I propose to break this general rule once, at this point. Could it not be the case that the masculine and feminine super-ego correspond to the features of castration as a threat (in relation to the father) and castration as a fact (founded in the much earlier relation to the mother)? Columnists, such as Linda Grant to whom I referred earlier, frequently complain that men are weak and stupid, that they can negotiate with their obligations as if they were a variable threat and that they let themselves off the hook precisely because duty seems so abstract, impersonal and neglectful of emotional considerations. In contrast, might it be that a woman, when she comes to it, experiences what she has to do as a fact, not negotiable at all but – to contradict Freud completely – as inexorable, just because it has taken emotions into account?

SEXUALITY DEFLECTED

Freud would have liked to define sexuality with the same precision as a doctor diagnosing tuberculosis. However, he had to face up to the difficulties of the masculine pathway, including the likelihood of psychic impotence, so that, as Freud says, even for a lucky male 'normal performance of the sexual function' is the result 'of a very complicated process' (1973–86, vol 10: 238). The same but more so for women, who must transfer from one sex to another and who are offered three different pathways, only one of which heads towards what Freud calls the 'normal female attitude' and even this, he says, is 'very circuitous' (1973–86, vol 7: 376).

Since the unconscious lies on the border between body and mind, potentially fixed definitions of sexuality become blurred as they are caught up and deflected through the world of meaning. I want to explore three ways in which the inescapable split between conscious and unconscious means that sexuality is 'disseminated', becomes (as it were) different from itself.

Perversion

The other animals, who are at one with their bodies, have a very limited range of sexual practices. We don't, as J.V. Cunningham describes:

> *Lip* was a man who used his head.
> He used it when he went to bed
> With his friend's wife, and with his friend,
> With either sex at either end.

> (1960: 91)

From the three possibilities ('oral', 'anal', 'genital') someone, somewhere, will have tried out all the combinations: oral/anal, genital/anal, oral/genital (some of these are more popular than others).

Mixing organs and sexes is only the beginning of what people get up to, as is notoriously evident from *Psychopathia Sexualis* published in 1886 by Richard von Krafft-Ebing three years before he became Professor of Psychiatry at Vienna. Besides homosexuality, sadism, masochism and exhibitionism, Krafft-Ebing (1965) lists the amazing number of objects people can use in amazing ways for sexual purposes: whips, chains, excrement, shoes, feet, hair (including underarm), statues, animals of all kinds (including ducks).

Ducks? A man was arrested for having sex with a Staffordshire bull-terrier beside a road in Bradford: he told the police 'I can't help it if it took a liking to me – he pulled my trousers down' ('This Life', *Sunday Times*, 6 December, 1998). Even training shoes can attract attention: 'Some guys are very much into jerking off with their sneakers, or using the sneakers in place of sexual anatomy' (American reported in 'All that is solid melts into Air Jordans', *Guardian*, 23 October, 1998).

Despite his enthusiasm for collecting perversions, Krafft-Ebing holds onto a distinction between 'normal' and 'perverse' sexuality (Latin *perversus*, 'turned aside'). Freud continues to refer to the possibility of normal sexuality, heterosexual genital satisfaction, and names as '"perversion"' (his scare quotes) any activity which: 1) extends beyond the designated bodily areas or 2) lingers on 'intermediate relations' that should 'normally be traversed rapidly' on the way to satisfaction (1973–86, vol 7: 62).

Which bodily areas are designated and how rapidly is normal? Isn't this a somewhat male-dominated view? Freud soon calls it into question, since he is committed to a belief that infants have sexual feelings, that all of us pass through oral, anal and genital pleasures, that we all have a potential to be 'polymorphously perverse'. Noting 'the extraordinarily wide dissemination of the perversions' he concludes 'that the disposition to perversions is itself of no great rarity but must form a part of what passes as the normal constitution' (1973–86, vol 7: 86).

Deferral

Again, how could sexuality be simply direct? How can we not linger on 'intermediate relations' unless we are like the man whose idea of foreplay was taking his socks off? Sexuality circulates through sight, touching, and kissing, an act so far from the sexual apparatus, Freud notes, that it actually uses 'the entry to the digestive tract' (ibid: 62) and so is by nature indirect or mediated. In any case, sexual desire is redirected by the Oedipus complex from the mother to another adult figure so that, as Freud says, every 'finding of an object [i.e. of desire] is in fact a refinding of it' (ibid: 145). This raises a delicate question since by definition what is 'refound', repeated, is not the same as it was the first time round, and the desire which takes it as its object must be – in the strict sense – 'turned aside' or perverse.

I have already mentioned the various substitutions through which the first, 'original' breast is refound, a series which begins with thumb-sucking and liquorice and goes on to Belgian chocolate, toffee, Bacardi and Coke, Château Latour. In fact, because of deferral there is not much that people do which doesn't have a sexual component – activities such as driving a car, looking at pictures in an art gallery, reading the sports pages in a newspaper, writing books on the unconscious.

Bisexuality

Freud affirms frequently, confidently and unequivocally 'the constitutional bisexuality of each individual' (1973–86, vol 11: 371), that 'bisexuality' is present 'in the innate disposition of human beings' (1973–86, vol 7: 374; see also: 52, 136, 142, 342). The choice of a sexual object from the opposite rather than the same sex is not given by nature but forms a temporary preference. Indeed, in times of crisis we can swap an object of one gender for another, as perhaps does a middle-aged man who turns from an active interest in women to drinking with his male friends at a rugby club or a pub. Such sublimated homosexual love, in men or women, is very important for reinforcing sympathetic feelings within groups (1973–86, vol 12: 176).

According to Freud, therefore, everyone has got not one but two ways of meeting the Oedipus complex: 'positive' (heterosexual) and 'negative' (homosexual). Faced with the threat of castration the little boy can confront his father and challenge him for access to the mother – the positive way which would lead to adult heterosexuality. Or, following the negative line, Freud suggests, the boy can try to avoid the threat by wishing to 'take the place of his mother and be loved by his father' (ibid: 318).

HOMOSEXUALITY

Homosexuality is already written into the script for so-called 'normal' sexuality. Male homosexuality, Freud mentions, was considered ordinary behaviour in Ancient Greece, even among those reputed to be 'the most masculine men' (1973–86, vol 7: 55–56). His research leads him to the view that 'all human beings are capable of making a homosexual object-choice, and have in fact made one in their unconscious' (ibid.), insofar, that is, as everyone is bisexual.

Male homosexuality originates in the childhood belief that everyone is phallic, including women, followed by the discovery that they are not. 'Probably no male human being is spared the fright of castration at the sight of a female genital' (ibid: 354) says Freud in his essay on 'Fetishism' where he also remarks that the fetish may save the fetishist (male) from 'becoming a homosexual' (ibid: 353–54) since it helps him to cope with a woman as a sexual object. The male homosexual, in Freud's analysis, is someone who turns away from women when he discovers that they are not phallic and becomes 'unable to do without a penis in his sexual object' (ibid: 194).

This response may coincide with the 'negative' side of a boy's Oedipus complex in which, at the same time as feeling ambivalent towards his father and affectionate towards his mother, the boy 'also behaves like a girl and displays an affectionate feminine attitude to his father' (1973–86, vol 11: 372). I say 'may coincide' because in the homosexual structure there are as many variations as in the heterosexual. For example, a further factor is introduced by identification, if a young man 'does not abandon his mother' at puberty but 'identifies himself with her' (1973–86, vol 12: 138).

Female homosexuality has been mentioned already, since it may follow from trajectory (2) offered to women, the girl who clings 'with defiant self-assertiveness to her threatened masculinity' (1973–86, vol 7: 376). This 'masculine complex', as Freud calls it, 'can also result in a manifest homosexual choice of object' (ibid.). In 'Femininity' (1933) he stresses that for both sexes what really matters in the belief that everyone is phallic is that it means the *mother* is phallic, the belief the male fetishist tries to preserve with his fetish. The female homosexual, therefore, refuses castration but also 'takes refuge in an identification with her phallic mother' (1973–86, vol 1: 164). Freud notes that homosexual women 'play the parts of mother and baby with each other as often and as clearly as those of husband and wife' (ibid.). Is this true? I don't know.

We live in a time when the Christian Fundamentalist right in the United States believes homosexuals are the spawn of Satan and can be 'cured' by just saying 'No!' and when in July 1998 the House of Lords in Britain voted against lowering the age of consent for gay men to sixteen. The House of Lords is full of ex-public-schoolboys who have probably got more homosexual experience than most of us (on ceremonial occasions they dress up in tights and buckled shoes). They were anxious to protect young men from the pleasures of the gay life which, it was feared, once tasted they might never want to give up.

Freud's view is more sanguine, as he explains in 'A Case of

Homosexuality in a Woman' (1973–86, vol 9: 371–400). A father, having discovered his eighteen-year-old daughter was having a homosexual affair, brought her to Freud, in fury, threatening her that if psychoanalysis did not cure her she would be sorted out by the next best thing, 'a speedy marriage' (ibid: 373). Freud soon broke off the treatment advising that she should try a woman analyst. 'In general', Freud concludes, 'to undertake to convert a fully developed homosexual into a heterosexual does not offer much more prospect of success than the reverse', though he adds that 'the latter is never attempted' (ibid: 376).

I don't want to leave Freud's argument here without trying to be explicit about something implicit in his theory of sexuality: he *needs* bisexuality. In a famous footnote of 1915 (1973–86, vol 7: 141) Freud defines gender in terms of: sociology (men and women); the body (male and female); the unconscious (masculine and feminine). In the end masculine resolves itself into 'active', feminine into 'passive' since libido is of 'a masculine nature' (ibid.), he says. This is borne out in the way that both the little boy and the little girl begin the same way, in actively and phallically seeking the mother. But doesn't that leave Freud with the problem of how women come about at all? Bisexuality gives some answer to that question. Freud could have argued that this originates from identification with two parents though in fact he does not.

LACAN: EITHER BEING OR MEANING

All of these questions around sexuality are rethought and recast by Lacan as an account of how the unconscious expresses itself in desire. As one would expect from what has already been said about his view of the unconscious, Lacan aims to integrate the analysis of sexuality with the operation of language. To begin to come to terms with his notion of sexuality and desire we need to grasp his general understanding of subjectivity and discourse. Lacan distinguishes between three orders – the real, the imaginary and the symbolic, which are knotted together. It has to be said that Lacan was eager that his writing should not be made over too easily by the mastering ego and should leave the reader only one 'way in', which, he says, 'I prefer to be difficult' (1977a: 146). Having noted this we can now consider more closely what the imaginary and symbolic involve.

The imaginary is the domain of the ego where the I mis-recognises itself as a full identity, imagines it speaks with clear and coherent meaning, but where it is in fact subject to all kinds of fantasy including the power to 'overlook' the symbolic order. The symbolic is the domain of culture, all the rules and symbolic meanings which exist 'out there' before I ever come along, especially, in Lacan's view, as a particular structure of signifiers, the Other. The real, for Lacan, is *there*, both inside us and beyond, outside language and resisting signification. In the real everything is simply itself, 'always comes back to the same place' (1977b: 49). The gaps and differences between the signifiers in language introduce lack and absence into the speaking subject; the real, in contrast, has no holes in it.

As human beings we start off as little animals, in the real, the world of being. My task, if I am to become a speaking subject, is to enter the symbolic order, the world of meaning which is waiting for me. In Lacan's view it is this transition from Being to Meaning which brings about the unconscious. He illustrates the relation of the two as a Venn diagram, two overlapping circles:

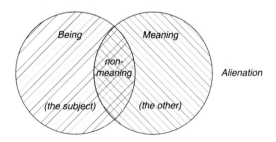

I think we may understand the shift from Being into Meaning as growing up, development from nature into culture, or in Lacan's terms, from the real to the symbolic. When I was born I was absolutely and completely myself, immune to any distinction between myself and the world. Entering the circle of Meaning, of language, which is the possession of other people, I begin to have a meaning.

Lacan phrases the either/or between Being and Meaning as a choice in which you lose either way – like the highwayman's '*Your money or your life!*' (1977b: 212). If I stay in Being I am completely myself but have no meaning; if I enter Meaning 'I identify myself in language', Lacan says, 'but only by losing myself in it like an object' (1977a: 86), for I can only say things which, in principle, *anyone* could say. In Being I am characterised by 'particularity' (ibid: 286) while in language I have to share the universality of the signifier. Language is 'universal' because it only works if it is a shared system so that any part of it can be used by anyone.

One problem with Lacan's illustration is that it is conceived from the point of view of someone who is *already* within Meaning. If I am within Being I am within Being; I am outside the process of signification, and I could not draw a diagram. So Lacan's model is really a model seen from a point of view after the transition. He asserts that 'the symbol manifests itself first of all as the murder of the thing, and this death constitutes in the subject the eternalisation of his desire' (1977a: 104). The symbol kills the thing because it replaces the self-defining real with an arbitrary term, the signifier. Within Meaning my 'Being' is lost 'like an object', because it becomes just like an item of language. Meaning therefore introduces what Lacan calls *manque à être* ('lack-of-being' or 'lack-in-being') into the subject.

However, 'every finding of an object is in fact a refinding of it' as Freud says (1973–86, vol 7: 145) – experiencing lack, I try to refind my being within meaning, a trace of that most intimate and particular me that was once there but got lost in the transition. In the diagram this seems to be shown as the cross-hatched area of 'non-meaning' which, Lacan says, 'constitutes, in the realisation of the subject, the unconscious' (1977b: 211). An example of the refinding of Being in Meaning might be Robert whose earliest self, tragically, reappears within language as 'Wolf'. Freud composes a more happy picture of Being as a baby 'satiated from the breast and falling asleep with flushed cheeks and a blissful smile' (1973–86, vol 7: 98).

NEED, DEMAND, DESIRE

The lack which cuts into the subject's being with language produces 'the eternalisation' of desire since desire is always desire for what is lacking. Lacan explains this development through three terms: need, demand and desire. There is little difficult with the concept of need; need is in the domain of the real, simply biological necessity. The infant's need for milk leads to a cry no different in principle from a kitten mewing for milk.

The most mysterious thing I have ever watched at close hand is a human being, day by day, learning to talk. For the new-born, language is a door closed on the other side – how *do* we ever get in? According to Lacan, what happens is that the infant cries for milk, makes the same awful, rending, unignorable noise, but at some point this develops from a signal to a sign. Lacan suggests it may take on the differential structure of the phoneme, to cry being distinguished from not crying. The sound acquires a human meaning, is not simply a *signal*, 'Milk now!', but a *sign* to another person: 'Milk now because you love me!'. Milk, the breast, has become 'a proof of love' (ibid: 286).

It would be wrong to think we experience lack and *then* language comes along and tries to make up for it. Language *produces* the very lack it tries to make good. Lacan refers to Freud's example of the *fort/da* game, and how a 'gap' or '*ditch*' opens at the edge of the infant's being as it plays with the cotton-reel, begins using the game to represent losing the mother (see 1977b: 62–63). It is the game that opens up the gap, 'a presence made of absence' says Lacan (1977a: 65). The signified seems to make meaning present though can only do so because of the operation of signifiers; though necessary to produce meaning, in themselves signifiers mean nothing. In this sense meaning is absent.

Demand

'Milk because you love me!': with demand, need starts to express itself in language and so is addressed to the other. Need is in the domain of the real, demand happens in the realm of the imaginary – it 'constitutes', says Lacan, 'the Other as already possessing the "privilege" of satisfying needs' (1977a: 286). A young child in a shop tries to get its parent to buy sweets, then a toy, then an ice-cream, howling inconsolably at each refusal. The child is not concerned with the real objects (if it gets one it wants another) but rather with what getting them means to it – 'Look what mummy's got me'. Demand is 'the demand for love' (ibid: 286). Interestingly, Lacan's biographer records that the young Jacques constantly asked 'for food or money or presents on the grounds that he was the eldest' (Roudinesco 1997: 7–8).

Unfortunately, demand outlasts childhood. When anyone takes personally something which is just neutral they are feeling it at the level of demand, especially when that demand seems disappointed. I miss the bus and curse the bus company, criminals would like to kill the judge who sentenced them. In the television sitcom *Fawlty Towers*, Basil has to collect food for a gourmet dinner. His car breaks down so he goes to the hedge, gets a stick and beats the car with the words, 'I've warned you'. He feels it has shown it doesn't really love him.

Desire

As my examples suggest, demand always fails to get what it wants and so gives way to desire. Demand spills over into desire when need drops out of the equation leaving a remainder: 'desire begins to take shape in the margin in which demand becomes separated from need' (ibid: 211). Or again, 'desire is neither the appetite for satisfaction, nor the demand for love, but the difference that results from the subtraction of the first from the second' (ibid: 287). So demand minus need equals desire – desire is in the symbolic, a structure of signification in which the real appears only as a trace or an effect.

Demand seeks a particularity – *my* need from *this* person. But it tries to do this in language, and language is by nature universal, so in consequence 'demand annuls the particularity of everything' (ibid: 286). Desire surrenders even this hope for particularity because it is enacted only within the universality of language. You find something you think signifies what you want only to discover it is linked to another signifier and another, within the Other (capital 'O').

Lack in being (*manque à être*) brings about desire ('desire is a relation of being to lack', Lacan 1988b: 223). Desire for a sexual object which is lacking is superimposed on this ('two lacks overlap', 1977b: 204). And though it sounds attractive, desire is not pleasurable but rather in excess of pleasure. While pleasure is controlled, contained within boundaries mapped out by the ego, desire cannot be held in place. Lacan says it crosses 'the threshold imposed by the pleasure principle' (ibid: 31).

Yet Lacan is sure that everyone's desire is somehow different and their own – lack is nevertheless *my* lack. How can this be if each of us is just lost in language like an object, floating in an infinite sea of signifiers? From all the possible signifiers why should I desire any one or any cluster of associated signifiers?

Passing through demand into desire, something from the real, from the individual's being before language, is retained as a trace, enough to determine that I desire here and there, not anywhere and everywhere. Lacan terms this *objet petit a* ('a' for 'autre', so 'object little other'). The algebraic formula is deliberately abstract, for two reasons. *Petit a* is different for everyone; and it can never be known except in *substitutes* for it in which I try to refind it. It is little 'a' because from all the signifiers of the so-called Big Other ('Autre'), my desire seeks out this one, as representing *my* object (for now).

Lacan asserts that 'desire is the metonymy of the want-to-be (*manque à être*)' (1977a: 259). Traditionally metonymy is a rhetorical figure in which one term stands for another associated with it ('The White House' for the 'American Presidency'). Lacan's notion of desire combines this idea of replacement with progression along the temporal line of a sentence. As they come along, desire tries out each signifier of a sentence – or a life – because it may stand in for *objet petit a*. But since at best each is never more than a stand-in, desire endlessly moves forward to the next term linked to it, the next likely object. In this respect the search for *objet petit a* is well exemplified in the series I have mentioned more than once – acid drops, vodka and lime, Haut Medoc, are all substitutes for the breast.

Except that for Lacan there is *no breast*, no first, original object, because, as he says 'the object' is 'the cause of desire, of that which is lacking' (1977b: ix). *Objet petit a* has a cause but all we can know of that cause is in the effects it produces – the cause does not lie somehow behind them or outside them. I think of this structure as the 'Lacanian Loop' and will come back to it in a minute with some more instances.

Much of Lacan's argument deals in abstraction. I can now try to offer some illustration of his general assertions. Gustave Flaubert's great novel of 1869, *Sentimental Education*, is the story of Frédéric Moreau in Paris in the mid-nineteenth century. On the fourth page of the Penguin edition (1964: 18) he meets Madame Arnoux, the wife of an acquaintance, and feels she is 'like a vision'. He decides he is in love with her and that 'the object of his existence was now clear' (ibid: 61). It might be remarked that Flaubert anticipates the psychoanalytic view that love is narcissism, for he comments immediately that Frédéric's face 'presented itself to him in the mirror' and 'he liked the look of it'. Though he has several other affairs, living through the 1848 Revolution in Paris and its bloody aftermath, he continues to see Madame Arnoux and remains faithful to her in his heart. Years later, five pages from the end of the novel (ibid: 415), she finally offers herself to him. Frédéric turns her down, fearing he would only feel 'disgusted', because, presumably, he would have to face the fact that the unattainable object of desire which gave his life purpose was just another surrogate for the real thing. For Lacan, of course, there can be no such real thing.

Another example. At one point Lacan specifies what *objets a* consist of – 'the breasts, the faeces, the gaze, the voice' (1977b: 242). Because, like music, someone's voice is simultaneously pervasive, invisible and unique we don't consciously notice it, and we have very few ways of annotating what makes it special. So it is well adapted to become an object of desire. If the television is on loud in another room you will instantly recognise someone's voice even if you can't actually name the person. All forms of singing, including opera and popular music, celebrate the power and pleasure of the voice; for example, in the rather strange movie, *Farinelli* (1994), a man brings a woman to orgasm by singing to her.

Singin' in the Rain (1952) is about Hollywood and the arrival of sound. A glamorous woman who plays lushly romantic roles in silent pictures suddenly has to talk. Unfortunately her voice turns out to be a squeaky, nasal whine with a Brooklyn accent. This ends her career. On the other hand, a current television advertisement, for mobile phones, shows clips of Martin Luther King – 'Ah have *seeeeeen* the Promised Land . . . I may not get there myself. . . .'. King's voice – resonant, seductive, arousing – could stand in for many people as *objet petit a*, which is why they used it in the advertisement.

Desire of the Other

Lacan states repeatedly that 'desire is the desire of the Other' (eg. 1977a: 264; 1977b: 235), exploiting the ambiguity of the French 'de' ('désir de l'Autre') which covers both desire *for* and desire *from*. Desire is of the Other in at least the sense that: 1) we desire because we are first desired – by the mother, by those whose image of us we internalise; 2) it can only emerge out there in the signifiers of the symbolic order; 3) desire is never for the same but always '*desire for something else*' (ibid: 167). An example: could it be that masturbation is generally less fun than sex with someone else because desire is of the Other?

Desire is an unconscious search for a lost object, lost not because it is *in front of* desire waiting to be refound but because it is already *behind* desire and producing it in the first place. Readers will have to make up their own minds about Lacan's theory. I would have to say that all my life I've thought that something would satisfy me and then, if I've got near it, discovered I wanted something else, and that this wasn't going to stop. As the song says, we keep trying because 'in another year we'll be happy'. Recognising that desire is without end and you can never get satisfaction helps keep you at a distance from yourself. Demand, with its unconditional insistence that the Other satisfy needs – *now*! – is childish and can only lead to unhappiness. However unsatisfactory, desire is grown up.

SEXUALITY IN LACAN

At last we come to Lacan on sexuality. But we have been there all the time because his analysis of sex presupposes the distinctions between need, demand and desire. Lacan rewrites the Oedipus complex via two terms – the Desire of the Mother and the Name-of-the-Father. What Freud thinks of as pre-Oedipal, Lacan describes as the infant seeking to be what the mother desires.

Freud asserts that 'nature has given babies to women as a substitute for the penis that has been denied them' (1973–86, vol 7: 297) and Lacan follows this view by asserting that 'If the desire of the mother *is* the phallus, the child wishes to be the phallus in order to satisfy that desire' (1977a: 289). We shall return shortly to the idea of 'being the phallus'. However, the mother desires more than the child as the phallus – perhaps she desires the father – so the child begins to feel he is not everything for her. As he or she experiences lack the dyadic mother/child relation becomes broken.

With the entry into lack, one signifier – the Desire of the Mother – is substituted for another, the Name-of-the-Father, in a process Lacan describes as 'metaphor' (ibid: 200). The Name-of-the-Father is the 'paternal metaphor', which in Lacan's version of *Totem and Taboo* (see below, pp. 138–40) must be recognised, he says, as 'the support of the symbolic function which, from the dawn of history, has identified his person with the figure of the law' (ibid: 67) – for Little Hans the Name-of-the-Father was 'horse'.

In French 'Name-of-the-Father' is 'Nom-du-Père'; when it is pronounced it sounds no different from the 'Non' of the Father. In Western culture another layer of meaning is added by the importance of the father's name in patriarchy. In Western society women have the surname either of their father or of their husband's father.

In the symbolic order the Name-of-the-Father introduces the subject to a name instead of a person, replaces someone real with a signifier. The father as a name where you might hope for the loving individual, encourages a child to move from demand to desire, from personal to impersonal. At some point everyone called on to play the father has to say something like 'Time to get up and go to school'; and in response to pleas of 'Oh, go on, five more minutes' has to say what authority figures always say: 'It's not up to me – those are the rules – get up and have your breakfast'. That is speaking in the Name-of-the-Father.

In *Reservoir Dogs* (1992) Big Joe (bald, besuited, deep-voiced, paternal) assigns aliases to the men preparing for a diamond heist: Mr. Orange, Mr White, Mr Blonde, Mr Blue, Mr Brown and Mr Pink. Mr Brown objects that his name sounds like shit; Mr Pink says his is faggoty and asks why they can't pick their own names. Big Joe refuses because they would all want to be Mr Black. Mr Pink offers to swap his name but is again stopped in his tracks. The implication is that the names are completely arbitrary, part of culture not nature, and for *that* reason fixed and non-negotiable. It is a striking instance of identity and the Name-of-the-Father which I have borrowed from a brilliant but as yet unpublished book on Tarantino by Fred Botting and Scott Wilson, *Holy Shit!*

Without coming up against the paternal metaphor a child might remain in the imaginary, in demand, in a world apparently without lack and limitation, the closed circle of childhood. The Name-of-the-Father says 'Here but not there', 'This but not that', giving the subject stability and position within language, a name, an identity which is no more (and no less) real than the name in Name-of-the-Father. The Name-of-the-Father 'sustains the structure of desire with the structure of the law' (1977b: 34).

The 'Lacanian loop'

I've already noted how Lacan contrives to put the cause or point of origin of *objet a inside* its consequences. He does something similar with the lack introduced by language: Meaning makes a cut into the self-sufficient circle of Being in a way which, through the power of coherent expression, promises to make up for the lack it has introduced.

Lacan offers us another loop when he considers Oedipus and Freud's view that finding is a re-finding, the mother is refound – repeated – in the adult sexual object. Lacan proposes that:

> The object is by nature a refound object. That it was lost is a consequence of that – but after the fact. It is thus refound without our knowing, except through the refinding, that it was ever lost.
>
> (1992: 118)

It is like going to a drawer and coming across something you'd forgotten about; refinding it makes you realise it was lost. Lacan loops the finding around the refinding so it becomes a *retrospective* effect. The object does not exist as a real cause outside the subject's fantasy. We will come across (refind?) a similar loop when the next chapter contrasts Freud's idea of fantasy in art with Lacan's.

'The Signification of the Phallus' (1958)

In this lecture (1977a: 281–91) Lacan gathers together many of his speculations about sexuality and language. He begins by pointing out the difficulties Freud gets himself into by not marking a clear separation between the body and the symbol, the penis and the phallus.

One difficulty is that though women can experience sexual pleasure from both the clitoris and the vagina, Freud gives precedence to the clitoris. He believes the first phase in boys and girls is phallic and so has to raise the clitoris 'to the function of the phallus' (ibid: 282). But he also has the problem that the phallus is manifestly symbolic rather than bodily, in the phallic mother, for instance, or the phallus the male fetishist continues to believe all women have. We will see whether Dr Lacan can do better.

As one might anticipate, Lacan's strategy is to assert that it is the signifier which castrates or imposes lack. Before language the infant can experience *jouissance*, a word which translates as 'orgasm' but in French has a stronger meaning altogether since it includes the idea of possessing something. It is perfectly expressed in Freud's suggestion of the 'blissful smile' on the baby satiated at the breast (1973–86, vol 7: 98). Such bliss is lost with the entry into language. '*Jouissance* is forbidden', writes Lacan, to anyone 'who speaks as such' (1977a: 319). What imposes castration, what forbids infantile *jouissance*, is the phallus and 'the phallus is a signifier' (ibid: 285). It is not just any ordinary signifier but 'the privileged signifier' (ibid: 287) which introduces the lack behind every other signifier.

Samuel Beckett was once asked what Godot symbolised in his play (*Waiting for Godot*) and replied that if he had known he would have said. The phallus is one of the most controversial notions in Lacan, and my own view is that if Lacan had known exactly what it was he would have said. Lacan wants the phallus to control two kinds of content: language (by designating 'the effects of the signified' (ibid: 285)), and at the same time sexuality (by promising it can get you *objet petit a* any time you want). He also wants it to be both present and absent, full and empty at once. What is certain is that for Lacan the phallus is not 'the organ, penis or clitoris, that it symbolises' (ibid.); any man who thinks his humble, workaday penis *is* the phallus is guilty of serious misrecognition.

The phallus as signifier has the function of marking sexual difference; with an unusual touch of diffidence Lacan murmurs, 'Let us say that these relations will turn around a "to be" and a "to have"' (ibid: 289). If she is prepared to try to 'be' the phallus for him, then he can imagine that in having her, he has it. Of course the more she pretends she is it and he has got it, the more he is reminded that she isn't and he hasn't. Love, says Lacan, is giving what you don't have.

In 'Like a Prayer' Madonna sings submissively that for her man she is 'Like a child'. For a woman to 'be the phallus', as is the child for the Desire of the Mother, means she has to 'reject an essential part of her femininity' in what Lacan calls 'the masquerade' (ibid: 290; see also 1977b: 193). The idea is taken from a paper by Joan Riviere, 'Womanliness as Masquerade' (1929), and makes the point directly that being the phallus (i.e. for him) is not the *whole* of femininity. Surely the familiar high-gloss, full-colour advertisements for cosmetics and clothes in women's magazines, which often show only isolated bits of a woman, illustrate unmistakably this notion of femininity as a masquerade?

The effect of the masquerade is to suggest he has the phallus, though this sounds less triumphantly patriarchal if you remember that having the phallus only gives him a signifier. Which means: 1) it isn't his; 2) he doesn't really have it; and 3) it won't satisfy anyone's desire (since desire cannot be satisfied).

The phallus

Lacan's 'privileging' of the phallus is not a metaphysical principle but an observation. The phallus is *contingent*, as Lacan implies when he says the phallus only acquires identity and content from the structure of fantasy; it is 'an essentially imaginary organ' (1982: 124). In principle, another signifier would carry out the function just as well: 'a certain society might decide to make a certain activity, quality or distinguishing mark a characteristic of man or woman, that is, a difference according to which men and women should be recognised' (ibid.). Something will always be needed to 'break the asocial dyadic unity of mother and child', as Juliet Mitchell argues (1982: 23).

Lacan saw it as his project to turn 'the meaning of Freud's work away from the biological basis he would have wished for it towards the cultural references with which it is shot through' (1977a: 106). Well, it is certain that for Lacan the phallus is not a bodily organ but one might query whether he really does any better than Freud at generating *two* sexes from his analysis. Why should a subject become a woman by taking up the position of being the phallus, especially if it means rejecting 'an essential part of her femininity'? In his so-called 'Diagram of Sexuation' Lacan has another take on these questions and does have something to say about this essentially feminine part. Before getting to Lacan's diagram I want to look at some examples, especially from women's writing, which might give an idea about 'the feminine'.

The 'diagram of sexuation'

We may recall that for Freud the masculine pathway is as follows:

little boy → mother → other adult woman

and the feminine equivalent is:

little girl → mother → father → other adult man.

That gives a basis for explaining why men are trapped with a Double Image of woman, the mother and the other woman, the Madonna and the Whore. Do women classify men into an ideal they love and disparaged figure they desire? The asymmetry of the pathways suggests that they don't – or don't so easily – because for women the mother and other object do not jar against each other directly. I want to pursue this a little by looking at some instances from novels and films.

Do women only have a single object? Emily Brontë's *Wuthering Heights* is one of the first novels ever to give a voice to women and it shows its heroine wanting *two* men. Catherine loves Heathcliff but marries Edgar Linton. Her decision is at the centre of critical debate – how could she do it? In fact, Catherine's plan is to marry Edgar without giving up Heathcliff. If she's not jealous why should they be? If they really loved her they'd put up with the situation. But they are trapped in the Double Image and can't cope with Catherine being loved *and* desired by both of them. The last page of the novel describes *three* headstones in the churchyard, for Catherine, Edgar, and Heathcliff together, as Patsy Stoneman argues in her fine analysis of the novel (see 1995).

Is Edgar Linton a father for Catherine, idealised and forbidden? Far from it, he's the other adult man who introduces her into marriage, children and society. Is it the other way round? Is Heathcliff the father, passionately and transgressively desired? But Cathy's feeling for him is not sensual and erotic – they walk the wild moors together, silent and ecstatic, but not actually doing very much.

A number of novels suggest that women have two objects. Dorothea wants Casaubon and Ladislaw (*Middlemarch*), Bathsheba wants Sergeant Troy and Gabriel Oak (*Far from the Madding Crowd*); for Tess there is d'Urberville and Angel Clare (*Tess of the D'Urbervilles*), for Sue Bridehead, Jude and Phillotson. In Lawrence's *Women in Love* Gudrun chooses Crick and Loerke. Virginia Woolf's Mrs Dalloway wants Richard Dalloway and Peter Walsh.

This is the case in novels, but also in film, including the most famous love-story of the twentieth century. In *Gone with the Wind* (1939), Scarlett O'Hara pursues both Ashley Wilkes and Rhett Butler. She does her best to persuade Wilkes to propose to her, is fiercely disappointed when he marries Melanie, and never really gives him up. But she also loves Rhett Butler, and they marry though in the end he leaves her.

Freud throws some light on the feminine 'double object' when he contrasts male and female sexual pleasure. A man has 'only one leading sexual zone, one sexual organ, whereas a woman has *two*: the vagina – the female organ proper – and the clitoris' (1973–86, vol 7: 374). The little girl generally does not know of the existence of her vagina and so treats her clitoris as source for sexual pleasure (Freud calls this a 'masculine' phase: ibid.). But in the process by which 'a little girl turns into a woman' (ibid: 143) she must give up clitoral activity and seek vaginal satisfaction instead. That is better because it promises her a husband and children. It is, Freud thinks, the correctly 'feminine' pathway (ibid: 374). So, the little girl has two possibilities for sexual pleasure and maybe two possible objects (whether Freud approves or not).

Lacan refers to male orgasm as 'the *jouissance* of the idiot' (1982: 152). Any man who's reasonably fair-minded will concede that his sexual pleasure is slight, superficial and brief compared to what a woman can experience: as the Waterboys sing, he 'saw the crescent' but she 'saw the *whole* of the moon'. Lacan picks up Freud's argument that feminine sexual pleasure has two sites, not one, but extends it into something much more profound. There is a sexual pleasure which circulates around the phallus but there is also another *jouissance*, her *jouissance*, which is 'beyond the phallus' (1982: 145).

Responding to this line in her book on Lacan, Jane Gallup calls Lacan a 'ladies' man'. Though phallocentric he is so concerned with pleasure that she reckons he exhibits the phallus to excess: 'in more pointed language, he is a prick' (1982: 36).

Lacan says he really doesn't know what this specially feminine *jouissance* is but compares it to spiritual ecstasy. In the Church of Santa Maria Vittoria in Rome there is Bernini's statue of Saint Teresa in ecstasy. Lacan says that Saint Teresa is experiencing *jouissance* but a *jouissance* that is not phallic:

> You only have to go and look at Bernini's statue in Rome to understand immediately that she's coming, there is no doubt about it. And what is her *jouissance*, her *coming* from? It is clear that the essential testimony of the mystics is that they are experiencing it but know nothing about it . . . I believe in the *jouissance* of the woman in so far as it is something more . . .
>
> (ibid: 145)

Freud believes women can have both vaginal and clitoral orgasm; Lacan theorises femininity as open to phallic *jouissance* as well as another, distinct *jouissance* which is 'something more', ecstatic, touching the beyond.

For Lacan sexuality is a *structure*, in the symbolic order, which is there before each of us comes along and where we have to find a position. Or positions. Although the two sides are diagrammed as exclusive, pure masculine and feminine do not exist; for example, someone who is biologically female must have some phallic function in order to speak:

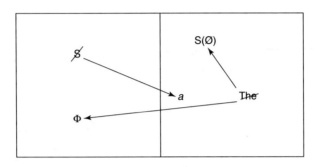

Masculine is figures on the left of the divide, feminine on the right. On the left there is the algebraic symbol 'S' with a slash through it. This is the barred subject, typically the man who is lacking and tries to find what will make up for it. Desire takes him along the arrow across the line into femininity and towards *objet petit a*. Desire also leads the man towards the apex of the vector on the feminine side where there is the barred 'The'.

'The' is 'The Woman', who, Lacan says, does not exist except as an idealised and universalised masculine fantasy, and this is why 'The' is struck through. The idealised woman and the disparaged woman are simply positive and negative forms of the same object, two sides of the Double Image. Masculinity is closed, as though all men wanted the same thing.

Femininity, on the other side, is open, defined in the drive towards two forms of *jouissance*. One comes from a desire to be what a man wants. Hence the arrow at the bottom, arising from the barred 'The' and passing across to the masculine side of the divide toward capital Greek *phi*, the phallus, which is *not* attached to barred S, the point of origin of masculine desire. Femininity may have phallic *jouissance* but there is also another possibility to be found by moving north-west towards 'S bracket barred O'. This is the site of a transcendental *jouissance* of her own, and it stays on the feminine side of the divide.

'S bracket barred O' is enigmatic. Elsewhere Lacan defines it as the 'signifier of a lack in the Other' (1977a: 316) and uses it to denote the moment of the subject's entry into language. He says we only have 'sporadic testimonies' (1982: 151) about what happens at this site, though he does speak of interpreting 'one face of the Other, the God face, as supported by feminine *jouissance*' (ibid: 147). This *jouissance* is turned towards the divine, the ecstatic, and remains mute and outside language, like Saint Teresa.

Is Lacan's account plausible? Consider two films. In *The Piano* (1993) the heroine is dumb, expressing herself (and her *jouissance*?) by playing her piano to herself – in one breath-taking sequence, on a beach by the empty ocean. Later she enters a sexual relation with a tattooed Harvey Keitel. She becomes torn between her desire for him and her desire for the piano; her husband cuts off part of one of her fingers to try to stop her playing and playing around. She loses this piano and gets another, ends up with Harvey Keitel, learns to speak.

In von Trier's *Breaking the Waves* (1996) a young woman lives in a remote island far north of Scotland; touched by madness, she has conversations with God. She falls in love with a man who works on an oil-rig; she is small and shy, he is huge and boisterous. After marriage he has to return to work and she is distraught, praying to God that he may come back to her at any cost. He does come back but only because he is paralysed in a terrible accident on the rig. He tells her that since he cannot make love any more she must make love with other men and tell him about it. She does, and finds it something, as she says, that she does 'very well' though the consequences are fatal for her.

However, the film ends with a mysterious affirmation, for after her funeral the thunder of church bells is heard from a clear sky.

One may ask what is going on here. Could it be that her relation with her God-like husband takes the form of ecstatic *jouissance* while her relations with the other men he sends her to represent phallic *jouissance*? Could it be that, from Catherine in *Wuthering Heights* to Scarlett O'Hara to the women in *The Piano* and *Breaking the Waves*, women are subject to not one but two forms of sexual delight?

If Lacan is right, however, one inescapable conclusion follows: that there is, as he says, no sexual relation. The two sides of the diagram are asymmetrical and there can be no possibility that what one wants the other can supply since they both desire different things.

One might say it is a dubious procedure to shift from novels and films to psychoanalysis and then back to texts. In the next chapter I will address explicitly the question of reading texts in relation to the idea of the unconscious.

5

THE UNCONSCIOUS AND THE TEXT

In taking the unconscious as its object for study psychoanalysis recognised it was working in an area traditionally the concern of art. Freud records that 'myths and works of imaginative writing and of art' are among those human activities 'whose connection with an incomprehensible unconscious was always suspected' (1973–86, vol 15: 180).

Literature or the unconscious? In the famous case history Freud retells Wolfman's dream:

'I dreamt that it was night and that I was lying in my bed. (My bed stood with its foot towards the window; in front of the window there was a row of old walnut trees. I know it was winter when I had the dream, and night-time.) Suddenly the window opened of its own accord, and I was terrified to see that some white wolves were sitting on the big walnut tree in front of the window. There were six or seven of them. The wolves were quite white, and looked more like foxes or sheep-dogs, for they had

> big tails like foxes and they had their ears pricked like dogs
> when they pay attention to something. In great terror, evidently
> of being eaten up by the wolves, I screamed and woke up.'
>
> (1973–86, vol 8: 259)

A little later he says what frightened him was that 'it seemed as
though they had riveted their whole attention on me' (ibid.).
How many wolves were there? 'There were six or seven', he says,
looking hard to try to work out whether they are wolves, foxes or
sheep-dogs. He draws a picture for Freud of the tree with the
wolves looking straight out (ibid: 260). There are only five of
them.

For the young child who had this nightmare it must have been
absolutely terrifying. For us, reading it second-hand, it comes
across like a scene from a film or novel. Where else might we find
such a powerful and uncanny effect as this dream of the walnut
tree and the white wolves with their pricked up ears and silent
gaze?

FANTASY

The common element between art and the unconscious is fantasy.
For psychoanalysis fantasy means: 1) an imaginary scene or
narrative; 2) in which the person fantasising is present; 3) but a
scene altered or disguised; 4) so as to fulfil a wish. Fantasy turns
ideas into concrete images and narrative; dreams work by '*the
transformation of a thought into an experience*' (1973–86, vol 1:
161). But art has always done this.

Fantasies are expressed in dreams and in art. The difference is
that actual, lived fantasies – day-dreams or night-dreams – can be
referred to the dreamer's life for interpretation, as Freud does with
the dream of the little girl and her 'butterfly' siblings (see above pp.
10–11). But art and literature cannot be referred to a particular,
individual dreamer.

Freud's ideas about art as fantasy change. At first he stresses the artist's or writer's own investment in fantasy but moves towards an interest in the *effect* of the artistic text on audience or readers. I have already introduced Freud's earlier ideas on art in 'Creative Writers and Day-Dreaming'. Art does two things. It provides disguised fantasies; and it does so by starting with a 'fore-pleasure', the purely formal features, which lead on to the fantasy. I will illustrate art as fantasy and then expand what Freud has to say about form, which is, he says, art's 'innermost secret' (1973–86, vol 14: 140).

DR NO

In thinking about creative writers Freud begins with popular culture – the less pretentious 'novels, romances and short stories' (ibid: 137). In each example he takes the centre of interest is a hero, and every hero is a survivor: 'If, at the end of one chapter of my story, I leave the hero unconscious and bleeding from severe wounds, I am sure to find him at the beginning of the next being carefully nursed and on the way to recovery' (ibid.). The true heroic feeling, Freud says, is expressed in the phrase, 'Nothing can happen to *me*' (ibid.).

There is a pay-off for the reader when they are given a feeling of security in identifying with someone who survives perilous adventures or a complex narrative. Freud concludes that 'His Majesty the Ego' is the 'hero alike of every day-dream and every story' (ibid: 138).

In Ian Fleming's 1958 novel, *Dr No* (filmed as the first Bond movie in 1962), Strangeways, a British agent in Jamaica, is murdered, and M sends Bond to investigate, warning him about Dr No and his guano-processing plant on nearby Crab Key. Arriving in Jamaica, Bond is sent a poisoned nectarine, which, of course, he doesn't eat, and attacked by a poisonous centipede, which doesn't kill him. He sails to Crab Key where he meets Honeychile on the beach – naked, alone, young, blonde, beautiful. They are attacked from a boat but escape. Then, Bond and Honeychile are captured by Dr No. Over an elegant dinner No explains that Honeychile will be exposed on the shore to the killer crabs and Bond will be executed horribly. Bond escapes and makes it to the sea where he fights and overcomes a giant squid. With a crane he buries Dr No under tons of guano. Honeychile, a child of nature, is nice to the crabs so they didn't touch her. She and Bond are rescued, he reports to M, she and Bond make love.

If readers identify with Bond, the text provides them with a powerful narcissistic fantasy. Though constantly threatened, his body resists coming to pieces. And the narrative shows him *almost* successfully making the Oedipal transition in winning Honeychile for himself. Almost successfully, that is, because Bond is a little too obedient to M, and so gets the girl only to lose her.

As so often in popular culture, the father is imagined as *two* figures: M the father for identification and No the castrating father. In the more recent film, *Star Wars* (1977), the split is between Obi-Wan Kenobe, 'you can be what you want to be', and Darth Vader, 'dark' or 'death father'. There seem to be two fantasy benefits. The hero is kept back from adult responsibilities that go with actually becoming the father; at the same time he can direct a very pleasurably justified aggression at the castrating father. This split is indeed a fantasy, because the father who castrates and the father with whom a man identifies are one. Fictional narratives, then, enact fantasies that provide unconscious pleasure.

THE PLEASURES OF THE SIGNIFIER

Even so, Freud thinks that the formal aspects of art automatically give us pleasure – rhythm and rhyme in poetry, narrative structure in a novel or film, visual aspects of painting or film, the specific sounds of music. I don't think there's much formal pleasure to be had from Fleming's novel. Having spent an evening with a painter,

Freud recorded in a letter that 'Meaning is but little to these men; all they care for is line, shape, agreement of contours'. They are, he concluded, 'given up to the pleasure principle' (Jones 1956–58, 3: 412). That pleasure – and ours – comes from the work/play of the signifier.

Freud claims that children find a special delight in 'treating words as things', as signifiers rather than meanings. In their collection of children's culture Iona and Peter Opie quote something they had heard in the school playground:

Mrs. White had a fright
In the middle of the night,
She saw a ghost eating toast
Half-way up the lamp post.
    (Opie and Opie 1959: 17)

The Opies comment rather pompously that this has 'neither wit nor reason to support it'. They've missed the point. As a nine-year-old told them, 'I think what's so clever about this is the way it all rhymes' (that is, sounds are repeated in 'White', 'fright', 'night' and so on). Freud would side with the nine-year-old. Adults want this pleasure of treating words as things too but have to disguise it from themselves, for example, in a song with a chorus of repeated sounds or a joke which depends on a pun. Freud suspects that the childish pleasure in playing with sounds is more fun than treating words as meanings: when 'we make serious use of words we are obliged to hold ourselves back with a certain effort from this comfortable procedure' (1973–86, vol 6: 168). The Teletubbies are not called John, Paul, George and Ringo, still less Matthew, Mark, Luke and John. They're Dipsy, Tinky Winky, Laa-Laa and Po.

In artistic writing the play of language gives pleasure in the same way as the rhyme about Mrs White. Freud refers to art's 'purely formal – that is, aesthetic – yield of pleasure' (1973–86, vol 14: 140). In my discussion the question of the signifier in art will keep coming up. But it will always trouble the argument because there just doesn't seem to be any way to integrate these formal aspects with the *meanings* art produces, signifier with signified.

In 1917 in the *Introductory Lectures* Freud offers another version of how the artistic text works (1973–86, vol 1: 423–24), beginning with a disabused account of the male artist as neurotic. Oppressed by 'excessively powerful instinctual needs', he desires 'wealth, fame and the love of women' but lacks the means to achieve them. Frustrated by reality he turns to fantasy, a path that would lead quickly to neurosis if the artist were not able to put his fantasies into a public form others could enjoy. He becomes a worldly success, as Freud remarks, and achieves through fantasy what originally he only had in fantasy – 'honour, power, and the love of women'.

Well, perhaps. But the psychology of the artist doesn't say much about art. In a long paragraph Freud now refers to three features which contribute to the successful aesthetic text:

1 There is a working of the signifier which links a 'large yield of pleasure to this representation' of fantasy; here the artist shows 'the mysterious power of shaping some particular material' so that 'repressions are outweighed and lifted by it'.
2 Fantasies are disguised, material from 'proscribed sources' toned down, the element of day-dream reworked so that it loses 'what is too personal' about it and begins to appear *impersonal*.
3 Embedded in a particular means of representation such fantasies become public and make it possible 'for other people once more to derive consolation and alleviation from their own sources of pleasure in the unconscious'.

Freud's emphasis is now on what art does for readers. The artistic text is successful if it makes it possible for others to share in the fantasies it holds out to them even though, in fact, each draws on his or her *own* unconscious sources of pleasure. Artistic fantasies are different for everybody but nevertheless something must be shared. The history of Hollywood would confirm this. Every year several hundred films are released, each hyped with expensive publicity. At the end of the year, certain movies have managed to provide pleasurable fantasies for a large number of people while others, the ones nobody talks about, have not. Maybe this principle can be extended across history: if a text from an older period doesn't continue to give pleasure it will risk being forgotten.

The account of art in relation to the unconscious can be divided into four different concerns: 1) the author; 2) the content of the text; 3) formal features; 4) the reader's experience. I shall take up each. Set out in advance they may look straightforward enough – in fact, each turns out to be problematic in its own way. On fantasy, for example, I shall digress at some length on differences between fantasy in Freud and in Lacan.

AUTHOR: LEONARDO DA VINCI

Freud believes that the artist is someone who diverts too much of their sexual energy into fantasy. His most sustained study of the psychic life of an artist is his short book on Leonardo da Vinci (1916). It is actually an analysis of the intellectual as a type, because Freud not only aims to explain such famous pictures as the Mona Lisa but also da Vinci's amazing scientific inventiveness. As one would expect, Freud's explanations relate back to da Vinci's experiences as a very young child.

Da Vinci's life is marked by the fact that he did not show signs of strong sexual feelings – passion, says Freud, had been converted 'into a thirst for knowledge' (1973–86, vol 14: 164). But not every kind of knowledge, since he was attracted narrowly to 'practically every branch of natural science' (ibid: 166), while something seems to keep him away from investigating the human mind.

Children go through a period when they ask endless questions: Freud says they want to ask 'where babies come from' (ibid: 168) but don't know how. Some people, those destined (or doomed) to become intellectuals, never get over this stage of question-asking. For an even smaller minority research becomes a substitute for sexual activity: da Vinci was one of them.

But how do we get from this position to the ambiguities of the Mona Lisa smile? Leonardo was a natural son, brought up by his mother, and then, before he was five, taken away from her and brought up by his father and his father's wife. Freud argues that this experience left Leonardo homosexual in his affections. He had a highly idealised image of his mother but the attachment turned him away from other women. His mother represented both 'the promise of unbounded tenderness' and 'sinister menace' (ibid: 209). It is that double meaning that we may find in Mona Lisa's enigmatic smile.

Da Vinci also painted the Virgin and Child with St Anne, the Virgin's mother. Although Anne is Mary's mother she is portrayed as little different in age from Mary and, remarkably, Mary is sitting on Anne's lap in such a way that the two figures become super-imposed. In the National Gallery in London there is a drawing of the same subject in which, again, the figures are fused in a strange way. The two faces are markedly different, with the Virgin smiling in maternal sweetness while Anne's look is undoubtedly sinister.

I hope this brief account suggests what criticism via the author's unconscious can do. A biography of the artist's own unconscious feelings can certainly produce a fabulous piece of interpretation. Whether it is right or wrong, Freud's extraordinary outline of da Vinci forces us to look closely at his masterpieces. But it is limited even according to Freud's own statement of how art works.

Da Vinci may or may not have had an over-close attachment to his mother which robbed him of heterosexual drive and this may or may not have led him to skew the smile of the Mona Lisa and paint the Virgin and St Anne together with peculiar intensity. However, this fails to suggest why his work should have been of any interest to the generations of viewers who have flocked to see the paintings and, who are deriving pleasure from the fantasies the images make available to *us*.

Nor does all of this alluring biographical narrative say anything about the *formal* features of da Vinci's work. Your mother could have made you a homosexual, you could have been fascinated with science and so on, but since the Renaissance that is a biography millions of young men have had. What da Vinci could do that they could not was work the paint on the canvas so that over the centuries millions of viewers have enjoyed looking at it. He had 'the mysterious power' of shaping his particular material into 'line, shape, agreement of contours', and of course, colour.

CONTENT OF THE FANTASY

A number of readings of fictional texts as fantasies have already rehearsed in earlier chapters. We have looked at Freud's analysis of *Oedipus the King*, as well as *Hamlet*, and at Lacan's discussion of that play. Freud also wrote an analysis of a short story by Wilhelm Jensen called *Gradiva*, and comments on *Macbeth* and Ibsen's *Rosmersholm*. Freud's account of what motivates Lady Macbeth is not very persuasive, concluding as it does that the problem of why she suffers illness after the murder of Duncan is 'insoluble' (1973–86, vol 14: 307).

He fares better with Rebecca West in Ibsen's *Rosmerholm*. Rebecca joins the household of John Rosmer as a companion to his sickly wife and seems to be responsible for encouraging her to commit suicide so that she can have Rosmer to herself. When he offers her marriage she refuses in horror. Freud finds her subject to incestuous feeling which he relates to the 'governess' fantasy – the young woman who enters a household and imagines the mistress disappearing so that she can take her place with the master. When Rosmer's proposal promises to fulfil this fantasy Rebecca's sense of guilt becomes overwhelming. In many respects Charlotte Bronte's novel *Jane Eyre* is another 'governess' fantasy.

In a spirit of enthusiastic homage, I have put forward a number of accounts of artistic fantasy along the way – in poetry by Blake and Ovid, novels by Orwell, Dickens, Jane Austen, Flaubert, as well as others in relation to the feminine 'double object'. We have also looked at films with attention to their fantasy content: *Carrie, Chinatown, Red River, Fahrenheit 451, Terminator 2, Now Voyager, Gone with the Wind, The Piano.*

There are, however, two main problems with trying to illustrate the analysis of an aesthetic text as fantasy. The first is that texts are different and the particular mechanisms of fantasy put to work are almost as different. Once the general point has been made that you can read art as expression of an unconscious wish, there is not much more to say. Second, content analysis always remains content analysis whether it is analysis of unconscious content or not. Discussion of fantasy leaves the 'innermost secret' of art untouched – its formal features.

In contrast to Freud, Lacan stressed the priority of the signifier in the operation of unconscious processes. It is disappointing, therefore, that his two best-known comments on literary works are basically concerned with content. His account of *Hamlet* takes little notice of the fact that Shakespeare has written a play, one shaped for the seventeenth-century English theatre, not a novel, poem or whatever. Lacan also has a long and fascinating inter-pretation of a short story by Edgar Allen Poe, *The Purloined Letter* (see 1972b). Again he shows little interest in its *writing*, an example in a popular genre, the detective story. Both these instances take the form of applied psychoanalysis; that is, the surface meaning of the text is discarded and the real meaning hidden underneath is revealed. Formal issues are set aside, as is the question of how different readers might respond to the text.

FORMAL FEATURES

Fantasy can appear in the content of aesthetic texts in many different versions. There are, however, at least as many uses of the signifier contributing to the pleasures of art. Art works through different perceptual modes (oral, visual, verbal, musical, sculptural), kinds (poems, novels, plays, films), genres (comedy, tragedy, thriller, adventure, drama). As well as this, in every text the means of representation has features specific to that text. So it is no easier to generalise about formal features than about content. I will give two examples as indications of how the work/play of the signifier adds to and *acts in with* other unconscious meanings, tragedy and the uncanny. And I will give a short discussion of the theories of Julia Kristeva about the unconscious and the formal aspects of art.

Tragedy

In 'Psychopathic Stage Characters' (1973–86, vol 14: 121–27) Freud advanced a number of conditions which help sad or tragic content in art give pleasure to the reader or spectator. You can identify with a main character who is noble even if they suffer; if they suffer you still have the reassurance that it is someone else on the stage, not you, and, further, that it is not real pain but fiction. In *Beyond the Pleasure Principle* Freud gives a more developed answer to the problem of why we enjoy watching tragedy.

Having described the *fort/da* game (see above: pp. 34–5), Freud decides that entry into language provides a degree of mastery for the child as compensation for 'instinctual renunciation' (1973–86, vol 11: 285). He turns this to the analysis of tragic art: 'artistic play and artistic imitation carried out by adults, which, unlike children's, are aimed at an audience, do not spare the spectators (for instance, in tragedy) the most painful experiences and can yet be felt by them as highly enjoyable' (ibid: 287).

In tragic art a loss stated in the signified meaning (the death of Hamlet) becomes a source of pleasure if the way it is represented gives a compensating mastery to the spectator, if language and representation are coherent, controlling, appropriately expressive. It is not much more than a paragraph in Freud but a very suggestive paragraph.

The Uncanny

Freud's essay on 'The Uncanny' (1973–86, vol 14: 335–76) rambles over interesting territory but I intend to concentrate on one definition he gives to 'uncanny'. A sense of the uncanny can occur when we feel that the repressed has come back. Specifically, there is a sense of the uncanny when something which used to be 'familiar and old-established' (ibid: 363) reappears in an alien form, when 'something *actually happens* in our lives which seems to confirm the old, discarded beliefs' of our ancestors (ibid: 371). Once-familiar ideas which have become foreign to us because of rational understanding may suddenly appear plausible again. We may find ourselves saying things like, '"So the dead *do* live on and appear on the scene of their former activities!"' (ibid.).

The effect of the uncanny in fiction depends on a particular working of the representation. Fairy stories are not uncanny, Freud says, because in them we expect miracles all the time. And it is the same with the 'supernatural apparitions in Shakespeare's *Hamlet*' (ibid: 373). But the situation changes 'as soon as the writer pretends to move in the world of common reality' (ibid: 374). The uncanny only occurs when 'old, discarded beliefs' are juxtaposed with modern reason within a *realist* narrative.

Cinema, which is very good at realism, is full of arresting examples of the uncanny. At the beginning of George Romero's *Night of the Living Dead* (1969) an average couple, brother and sister, drive through a bleak landscape to a deserted cemetery to leave a memorial on their father's grave. As they remark, it is still strangely light at 8.00 p.m. While they are talking, a member of the living dead comes towards them, with the ungainly steps of a Boris Karloff monster; he attacks the woman and kills the man. The woman runs off. The powerful effect of the uncanny in this scene could not take place without an equally strong sense of 'material reality' (ibid: 375) – an everyday presentation of the modern world with cars, people wearing ordinary clothes and smoking cigarettes.

Formal features: Kristeva

People always seems to want to talk about pleasure. What form of textuality makes literature enjoyable has been explored in psychoanalytic terms by Roland Barthes and in relation to feminist theory by another contemporary French writer, Julia Kristeva. Barthes draws on Lacan's distinction between *pleasure* and *desire* (see above: p. 94) to discriminate two states of feeling that may be aroused by a text:

> Text of pleasure: the text that contents, fills, grants euphoria; the text that comes from culture and does not break with it, is linked to a *comfortable* practice of reading. Text of bliss: the text that imposes a state of loss, the text that discomforts (perhaps to the point of a certain boredom), unsettles the reader's historical, cultural, psychological assumptions, the consistency of his tastes, values, memories, brings to a crisis his relation with language.
>
> (1975: 14)

Roughly, the text of pleasure is represented by a conventional realist text – George Eliot's *Middlemarch* might be an example; the text of bliss (that is, *jouissance*) is more likely to be a Modernist work, such as Joyce's *Finnegan's Wake* or Godard's movie, *Wind from the East* (1967), both of which can indeed discomfort to the point of boredom, as Barthes says, but also have stunning moments you would never come across in a normal, everyday pleasurable text.

For her account of textual pleasure Kristeva also finds a source in Lacan, though a different one. Instead of Lacan's distinction between the imaginary and the symbolic, Kristeva distributes that material to give a quite new evaluation of the formal and phonetic force of language, as well as their unconscious effects (see Kristeva 1974). She assigns the communicative, systematic, homogenous and coherent aspects of signification to the *symbolic* (in her definition of it); and reserves for the *semiotic* a range of linguistic effects particularly characteristic of poetic language.

These include phonemic repetitions, evident in rhythm and rhyme, in addition to the gaps and dislocations in coherent discourse which Lacan regards as an opening in which the unconscious manifests itself:

> the *semiotic disposition* will be the various deviations from the grammatical rules of the language; articulatory effects which shift the phonemative system back towards its articulatory, phonetic base and consequently towards the drive-governed bases of sound-production; the over-determination of a lexeme by multiple meanings . . . syntactic irregularities such as ellipses, non-recoverable deletions, indefinite embeddings, etc. . . .
>
> (Kristeva 1992: 78)

We have previously come across words (lexemes) with several meanings; ellipses are sentences with parts missed out ('Beer, please' instead of 'I would like to have some beer'); non-recoverable deletions are words lost for ever from a text; and embedding is a syntactical construction in which clauses depend on other clauses until the reader can get a bit confused (embedding is, in fact, a feature of Lacan's own style).

For Kristeva the semiotic is pre-Oedipal. Insofar as the pre-Oedipal mother is imagined as having masculine and feminine attributes, maternal *and* phallic, so also is the semiotic. The semiotic is present as a possibility in all discourse, and its articulation within and against the symbolic can have a political effect (in her study of 1974 Kristeva instances the work of the French late nineteenth-century avant-garde, including the strange poetic prose of the Comte de Lautréamont and the poetry of Stéphane Mallarmé).

What is crucial to this analysis is that Kristeva's semiotic is not an expression of some essence of the feminine, a charge that can be levelled against the conception of *écriture féminine* put forward by such writers as Hélène Cixous and Luce Irigaray (see Moi 1985). Rather, the semiotic has a marginal and disruptive impact which works against the grain. It takes on a progressive potential because it can put in question the dominant masculine forms, with their claims to clarity, unity and homogeneity.

Kristeva's account of the semiotic is not without problems. Does the semiotic in fact exist at all with the unconscious meanings she thinks it has? Is it plausible to define the semiotic as compre-hending both dislocations in language and forms of phonemic repetition? And can repeating sounds, in rhythm and rhyme (or even something within them, at the very edge of actual represen-tation) really have the subversive power Kristeva describes?

This last is not Freud's view at all: 'It is generally acknowledged that rhymes, alliterations, refrains, and other forms of repeating similar verbal sounds which occur in verse, make use of the same source of pleasure – the rediscovery of something familiar' (1973–86, vol 6: 170). Far from thinking it radical and unsettling, he regards verbal repetition as pleasurably reassuring. Neverthe-less, Kristeva's intervention brilliantly focuses attention on what is so often disregarded in aesthetic questions, the formal aspects of signification. At the centre of human life both Freud and Lacan recognise the ultimately undefinable activity in which represen-tation is produced, working on the very stuff and material which leads to meaning.

ART AND THE READER

In the 1960s' review, *Oh Calcutta*, there is a sketch, supposedly contributed by John Lennon, in which six men masturbate, with their backs to the audience, while their fantasies are revealed one by one on a big screen in front of them. Five of them are imagining naked women in seductive poses – but the sixth is thinking about a gorgeous naked male. Once you start asking about what *actual* fantasies readers people find in art there is simply no limit.

Take a fairly straightforward genre text such as *Dr No*. I might identify with Bond as the text seems to want me to. But what happens if I'm a woman? Do I go to sleep except when Honeychile is on the screen? Or if I'm gay? Who do I identify with and who do I desire then? How does a child feel watching the film? If I have been to Jamaica on holiday recently I am likely to have special associations with the blue skies and tropical beaches. Or suppose I'm particularly turned on by anal pleasure – the death of Dr No under tons of bird-shit is going to affect me in ways other people will not necessarily share.

There is no way in which it is possible to draw a respectable line between individual fantasies that are appropriate to the text and others which are not. The artistic text does not pass *its* pleasures across to the audience but allows people to find 'their *own* sources of pleasure in the unconscious' (my italics). The best we can say is that a common set of *signifiers* is available to different individuals and each responds to these. The fact that some texts are read more often and more widely than others is evidence for a ground common across individual readings.

The idea of the unconscious has encouraged critics to try to talk about the pleasures of *actual* readers (the work of Norman N. Holland is a good example, see 1968 and 1975). But such accounts end up being either the fantasies of that particular writer, which are not very interesting, or they write about what they see as *the* fantasy contained in the text, which is a little more interesting.

There is no escape from this dilemma. There is, though, a very important way of thinking about the question, even if it does not resolve it. This concentrates on the reader as identifying with a *position* offered by the text, a position which can be discussed seriously but which is, in principle, open and variable. Developed more completely in film theory than anywhere else, that approach begins by rejecting Freud's conception of fantasy and embracing Lacan's reworking of it (see Laplanche and Pontalis 1968). We need to understand the difference between the two. This becomes clear when both Freud and Lacan interpret the same dream.

FANTASY IN FREUD AND LACAN

Below is one of the most moving dreams Freud ever records (another of the psychoanalytic texts it would be difficult to match from literature):

> A father had been watching beside his child's sick-bed for days and nights on end. After the child had died, he went into the next room to lie down, but left the door open so that he could see from his bedroom into the room in which his child's body was laid out, with tall candles standing round it. An old man had been engaged to keep watch over it, and sat beside the body murmuring prayers. After a few hours' sleep, the father had a dream that *his child was standing beside his bed, caught him by the arm and whispered to him reproachfully: 'Father, don't you see I'm burning?'* He woke up, noticed a bright glare of light from the next room, hurried into it and found the old watchman had dropped off to sleep and that the wrappings and one of the arms of his beloved child's dead body had been burned by a lighted candle that had fallen on them.
>
> (1973–86, vol 4: 652)

Freud's reading is not complicated. The idea of burning comes from the fallen candle – and perhaps from words spoken by the feverish child before he died. The dream contains the fulfilment of a wish for 'the dead child behaved in the dream like a living one' (ibid: 653) – he's still alive. The dream is prolonged by this and another wish which is the father's 'need to sleep' (ibid: 726).

Lacan disagrees. In doing so he draws on his own idea of fantasy as the effect of the imaginary as well as his rather difficult notion of the real as that which lies outside representation altogether. For Lacan, the content of the dream – the child who is burning – corresponds to 'what is happening' (1977b: 57), the overturned candle setting light to the bed. This hardly confirms 'that the dream is a realisation of desire' (ibid.). Second, granted that the father wished to sleep, what woke him up? 'Is it not, *in* the dream, another reality?' (ibid: 58), Lacan asks, something in the child's gesture of taking him by the arm and his whispered question, '*Vater, siehst du denn nicht dass ich verbrenne?*'.

What can the question mean unless it is a reproach to the father for *not* seeing, not caring? The words 'perpetuate the remorse felt by the father'; they embody 'the missed reality that caused the death of the child' (ibid.) though this cause is not represented except by the gesture and the words. So, 'desire manifests itself in the dream by the loss expressed in an image at the most cruel point' (ibid: 59). Lacan does not deny elements of wish-fulfilment registered by the fact that the child appears alive, but he does affirm that overall the dream is not the realisation of a wish. Rather, it contains within itself the lack the fantasy tries to mask. This is another one of those 'Lacanian loops' referred to earlier (see pp. 99–100).

Freud regards fantasy as the fulfilment of a wish. Lacan sees it as a narrative which stages desire. For Freud, you and the fantasy are separate – wanting something you don't have you *then* try to satisfy that wish in fantasy. Not so in Lacan. The fantasy *brings about* the lack which makes the fantasy desirable. For Freud you are outside the fantasy, for Lacan you are an *effect* of the fantasy – in a sense you are your fantasies.

This allows Freud to describe the artistic text with a general confidence about what wishes it fulfils, and, to be fair, that is pretty well what Lacan himself does in reading *Hamlet*. However, Lacan's idea of fantasy moves beyond this. Lack is not simply present in the subject as a wish with the text as its fantasy fulfilment. Lack and fantasy produce each other so everything presented in the whole scenario incites a desire it is meant to satisfy. Who can say how or where anyone will latch onto the text? It depends on how the reader identifies with it. There are therefore *multiple points* for identification.

MULTIPLE IDENTIFICATIONS: BEING BEATEN

Training a dog is relatively straight-forward – you punish it for bad behaviour and reward it for good. This treatment just does not work with human beings because to some extent we all enjoy punishment and feel uneasy at being rewarded. Every evening you can turn on television and watch scenes of someone getting beaten – hit with a chair-leg, punched, kicked, slapped, tortured, hurt. Why is this heady mix of sadism and masochism going out night after night unless people are getting off on it?

Freud suggests such pleasures begin in childhood, with a fantasy expressed in the little scenario, 'A child is being beaten' (see 1973–86, vol 10: 159–93). The point is that simultaneously this provides *different positions* for people to identify with. In the first the beating-fantasy is represented by the phrase, '*My father is beating the child*' (ibid: 170); in the next the equivalent wording would run, '*I am being beaten by my father*' (ibid: 170); and in the third 'I am probably looking on' (ibid: 171).

What is agreeable about the first position is the idea that 'My father does not love this other child, *he loves only me*' (ibid: 172). The second, '*I am being beaten by my father*', would be very suitable for expressing a girl's incestuous impulses towards her father. He is punishing her for her love for him according to the perverse logic of the unconscious, which can be formulated as: if I'm being punished, I must have wanted to do it.

In the third the subject appears 'as a spectator' (ibid: 176) and a teacher is beating a number of children. The subject is a bystander, the role of the beater is played by a third person, a teacher or figure of authority, and this greater disguise of personal motives allows it to become the most charged and erotic of all the versions. For the same reason it promotes a number of variations, including, for boys, '*I am being beaten by my mother*' (ibid: 186), and for girls, '*I am being beaten by my father*'. From this one might turn aside for a moment to draw a moral for parents: try not to smack a child for *anything* because it will always go too deep and mean the wrong thing.

'A child is being beaten' illustrates the fact of multiple positions in and for a scenario. However, these do not correspond directly to those brought about by identification with a fantasy narrative. In the Vietnam film, *The Deer Hunter* (1978), after Mike and his two friends have been captured, the Vietcong commander forces the prisoners to play Russian roulette with a loaded revolver. Those who refuse are thrown into bamboo cages in the river where they drown. The scene is so harsh it is almost unwatchable. There are various positions for a viewer to identify with if they see it through.

I identify with Mike and his friends forced to kill themselves, a position of narcissistic sympathy and heroic pathos. Then, whether I want to or not, I identify with the authority and aggression of the Vietcong commander. It is because identifying with the commander kicks against identification with the victims that the scene produces anxiety. Contradictory feelings could be held in place by a third point for identification, the spectator watching, and this might reassure me that I am safely outside the events of the story. Does it with this scene? The tensions set up here are so strong they are only relieved when Mike kills the commander and leads an escape. Arguably, we want it so much we don't notice how implausible it is.

This argument about the ambivalences of identification poses a real problem for high-minded, moralistic and well-intentioned authors who present us with scenes of physical violence and cruelty to show us how wrong it is. While I would certainly not disagree with this it must be the case that we are also going to find unconscious pleasure where we are not meant to. In *Uncle Tom's Cabin* we are aware of righteous anger at the scene in which Tom is brutally flogged. But the idea of the unconscious insists (to our discomfort) that we also identify *masochistically* with Tom and *sadistically* with the man doing the beating. In *Schindler's List* (1993), against all our better ideas of ourselves, we may well identify with the sleek mastery of Goeth, the Nazi officer, when he lounges on his balcony in his braces smoking a cigarette as he picks off Jews in the neighbouring camp with his high-powered rifle.

It can be said, of course, that we could not possibly identify with a sadistic monster like Goeth. However, there is evidence that the immediate context, especially his relationship with his Jewish house-servant, is constructed to ensure that we do find Goeth deeply unpleasant. In addition, there are sequences in Hollywood movies such as *Point Blank* (1966), *Targets* (1967), and *Dirty Harry* (1971) in which looking through the telescopic sights of a sniper's gun seems designed to encourage identification.

FANTASY AND PLEASURE IN THE TEXT

'Desire is the metonymy of the want-to-be' says Lacan's lapidary epigram. Desire is the effect of lack, lack of *objet petit a*, which is pursued through a metonymy of substitutions for it. The problem of the reader and the aesthetic text can be approached on the basis of Lacan's account of fantasy as the setting out of desire, especially if the text takes the form of narrative in which – metonymously – one event is linked to the next.

Desire is *created* by the text. As Lapsley and Westlake point out, 'before entering the cinema the spectator does not care whether or not ET calls home, or the towering inferno is extinguished' (1993: 191). If I actively make sense of the text I come to care about what the text cares about. Its lack becomes my lack, its desires my desire.

This is why artistic texts can give pleasure:

> In the cinema, however, there are times (perhaps infrequently) when it seems that there is nothing left to desire, when everything demanded of the text seems to have been gratified. That this can be so is because the text itself has determined the nature of that demand in such a way that the desires that emerge can apparently be satisfied. . . . Just as in the Hollywood romance the couple seem made for one another, so too the film and the spectator.
>
> (Lapsley and Westlake 1993: 191).

Aesthetic texts in general, not just film, give pleasure by exciting the desires they appear to satisfy.

PSYCHO

To suggest in detail how desire and identification may work in a text I shall take the example of Hitchcock's film *Psycho* (1960), a film with which almost everyone is familiar. Marion Crane is having an affair with Sam Loomis but he can't afford to marry her. She steals $40,000 from her employer and drives off to join Sam, stopping halfway at the Bates Motel. She meets the son of the owner, Norman Bates, and hears his mother shouting cruelly at him in the old house behind the motel. Resolved to return the money, she takes a shower. A figure with a huge knife enters and kills her. Norman finds the body and cleans up all traces of what his mother has done.

Lila, Marion's sister, goes to Sam Loomis thinking Marion is with him. They are interrupted by a detective, Arbogast, sent to find out what has happened to the $40,000. Finding the Bates motel, Arbogast goes into the house and is murdered. In pursuit of Arbogast, Lila and Sam talk to Norman, then go to the sheriff. They return to the motel. While Sam keeps Norman talking, Lila goes into the house to talk to Mrs Bates. Norman comes back, so she hides in the fruit-cellar – where she discovers the mummified body of Mrs Bates. Norman attacks her but she is saved by Sam. Norman is arrested. A psychiatrist explains: Norman killed his mother and her lover, then stole his mother's body and preserved it. Dressed as his mother he killed women who visited the motel.

We like to think aesthetic texts are formed into a seamless unity but they aren't. *Psycho* is full of gaps and juxtapositions. To begin with, there are two main narratives, not one. Marion's story has no necessary connection with her death; it is pure chance she stayed at the Bates Motel. Her death initiates a second narrative, the investigation of her disappearance. We have two narratives; and a main character who is not one but two people. But we don't find this out until near the end. If we knew earlier then Lila's wandering round the house would not give rise to the anxiety that she will meet Mrs Bates armed with a knife. There is also a discontinuity between the events as we follow them and the events as we reinterpret them afterwards, just as in *Oedipus* the king only finds out retrospectively that he has killed his father and married his mother.

We don't care what happens to Marion Crane until we are caught up in the film. Marion lacks a sexual relation and thinks she can get it ('Oh Sam, let's get married!') if Sam can pay off his debts. After hesitating, she steals the money from Cassidy, an overbearing and disturbing father-figure. We certainly take Marion as a point of identification, though everything that happens to her after taking the money warns that her desire cannot be fulfilled: she sees her boss at a pedestrian crossing, hears accusing voices in her head, is woken by a sinister policeman after sleeping in her car, is accompanied by ominous music on the soundtrack. It is a relief when, having listened to Norman explain how he lives with unrealised desire, trapped by his obligation to his mother, she decides to give the money back.

But it is too late. No popular film before *Psycho* had ever eradicated a famous leading lady after only forty minutes. This, our strong identification with Marion, and the sudden, awful violence of her death, introduce a sense of lack so powerful we will follow the rest of the film wanting it to be made good, to know why she died, and for her killer to be brought to justice. The dark figure glimpsed through the shower curtain as it enters is like the boy who appears and touches his father's arm in that dream. Though present on the screen it imports a sense of the real beyond representation.

There are few better examples to show the role of identification in aesthetic texts than what happens next. If we are to stay in our seats we must switch from Marion to Norman. This has been anticipated when they get on so well: he asks, 'We all go a little mad sometimes – haven't you?'. He is charming, boyish, shy, and honourable – wouldn't hear of his mother being put in an institution. Though he tries to limit his own desire he does spy on Marion in the shower; after her death, though, he is overcome with desire to save his mother ('Mother! Oh God! Mother! Blood! Blood!').

Overlapping with these other desires, for better for worse, we cannot fail to find Mrs Bates a point of identification. She is the phallic mother, raising her huge knife again and again over the prone body of Arbogast. Furiously sarcastic ('Do you think I'm fruity?'), wholly self-concerned (that voice!), she embodies in psychotic form the Desire of the Mother and kills Marion from a wish to keep her son all to herself. The Slovenian critic Slavoj Žižek suggests that if Marion's journey is presided over by the Name-of-the-Father, the other two-thirds of the narrative imply the Desire of the Mother (see 1992: 226–31).

And surely we recognise that house, only too well, and have a charged yet uneasy identification with it? This is mother's house, the old, gloomy, clapboard house on the hill, familiar from the horror tradition, with its curlicues, Victorian decorations and stifling old-fashioned furnishings, the bedrooms, the nursery, and below stairs, of course, the cellar. In dreams a typical representation of the human figure 'is a *house*' and those 'with projections and balconies that one can hold on to are women' (1973–86, vol 1: 186). The house is uncanny, a place which makes 'old, discarded beliefs' believable alongside the 'common reality' of the motel.

Suspense is sustained in the rest of the film through the conflict between two desires: for Norman to guard his secret and for the death of Marion to be put right. The second wish is supported by new figures who enter the plot, such as Lila and Sam, Arbogast the detective, the local sheriff. In one sense that desire is satisfied by the conclusion of the narrative though in fact none of the resolutions is really complete. In fact, there may be as many as *four* possible conclusions.

The first ending comes with the finding of the body in the cellar and the recognition that Mrs Bates is Norman. Learning that Norman killed Marion makes Norman an extreme example of the man who can love or desire, and who kills the thing he desires. This re-reading overrides what we experience during the course of the narrative but cannot annihilate it. The two interpretations – Mrs Bates is Mrs Bates and Norman is Mrs Bates – support each other in expressing a forbidden wish for the mother/infant dyad. But the full compulsion of Norman's desire only appears after the event, in the cancelled version, which, like desire itself, is lacking, fugitive and displaced. What we thought he was saying at the time, and what we now realise he meant, are split as conscious from unconscious. It is only in retrospect, sliding away from us, that we glimpse why he told Marion that his hobby was 'stuffing birds' or that 'a boy's best friend is his mother' or, as he tells Sam Loomis, 'I had a very happy childhood – my mother and I were *more* than happy'.

There is a second ending when the psychiatrist explains that Norman killed his mother. The glib tone of this speech signals that it is limited, for it gives only a rational understanding, 'word presentations'. In a third ending Norman, draped in a blanket, sits quite still while his mother speaks in voice-over until his smile is superimposed on her skull. At this point they are now indeed one. The image is uncanny, the 'discarded' idea of demonic possession. Unnervingly, it also recalls the smile on Marion's face as she drove to the motel and imagines the man she had stolen from shouting that he would replace any missing money 'with her fine soft flesh'. Norman's look at us, at the camera, seems to say he knows everything but tells us nothing. A final shot of Marion's white car dragged from the black mud suggests things being put back in place.

But are they? These endings tend to show that desire cannot be brought to an end. We can know what happened to Marion (the psychiatrist's explanation) but unconscious desire outruns any such knowledge. A text gives pleasure because it incites only desires that can apparently be satisfied, as Lapsley and Westlake argue. But texts do more than give pleasure. If Lacan's analysis of fantasy is right then the interest or charge in a fictional text may come as much from the very *fact* of staging or setting out of desire as from any imaginary realisation of it.

6

THE UNCONSCIOUS
AND HISTORY

So far, the concern with the unconscious has been with the inner psychic life of individual human beings, though it has already had to move beyond this when considering art and the unconscious. This present chapter aims to expand the scope of the discussion in order to argue that the unconscious acts as 'lining' or 'inside' to all forms of social life. I will conclude by looking at what psychoanalysis thinks people are like, an attitude which some may find bleak while it strikes others as simply unsentimental.

UNIVERSAL HUMAN NATURE?

The social sciences usually assume that the materialism of historical explanation and the metaphysical idea of the unconscious are mutually exclusive. A classic statement of this attitude is Durkheim's famous remark, 'Whenever a social phenomenon is directly explained by a psychological phenomenon, we may be sure that the explanation is false' (cited in Jameson 1977: 339).

John Breuilly typifies the attitude of many historians when he writes in *Nationalism and the State* that any attempt to consider the feeling for nation in terms of 'the need for identity' should be immediately rejected on the grounds that it 'posits a universal, non-rational entity' (1982: 33). Traditional Marxism shared this view, and Raymond Williams represents it well when he denies that 'Freud and Marx could be combined' because 'there can be no useful compromise between a description of basic realities as ahistorical and universal and a description of them as modified by a changing human history' (1979: 184).

The first thing to be said is that while Jung saw the human psyche as ahistorical and universal, Freud did not. Jung came to believe that psychic energy expressed itself in certain special symbols and that these images or 'archetypes' exist in very much the same way across human history in the form of a 'collective unconscious'. The individual is made up of a particular mix from this universal material. If we go back to Freud on the interpretation of dreams, it is clear his conclusion is different.

Freud accepts that dreams express themselves in an inter-subjective symbolism, though remains open to the possibility that this is local to a given culture. But he insists that every dream is personal and has to be understood in the particular context of the individual dreamer's experience and unconscious disposition. This experience can never be solitary.

At the beginning of *Group Psychology and the Analysis of the Ego* Freud argues that the contrast between the individual and the social should not be overemphasised. Individual psychology is concerned with the individual and their search for satisfaction. But 'in the individual's mental life someone else is invariably involved, as a model, as an object, as a helper, as an opponent; and so from the very first individual psychology' in this extended sense 'is at the same time social psychology' (1973–86, vol 12: 95). A similar view is much stronger in Lacan's account of the dependence of the individual subject on a pre-existing order, the symbolic.

Along the way I have given a number of examples to support the claim that our identity is profoundly shaped by our earliest experiences and that these are experiences with others. To the sad story of Robert, the young boy who could only say '*Miss!*' and '*wolf!*' (see above, pp. 71–72), we might now add the question of how Norman Bates (admittedly fictional) came to be who he was. His father died when he was young, depriving him of both a model and an opponent, he had no brothers and sisters, he lived in isolation, and therefore everything drove him back into the mother/son dyad.

FREUD AND HISTORY

History is not the concern of a theory of the unconscious. But Freud does envisage a historical progression in the slow headway made by civilisation. The animism of the earliest people in which every human interest is seen as involved with the supernatural has given way to modern science in which, in principle, everything people do can be given a material explanation. Far from being utopian, this progress includes loss as well as gain. Comparing *Oedipus* with *Hamlet*, Freud points out that in the first the incestuous fantasy is 'brought into the open' as it would be in a dream while in *Hamlet* we only learn of existence indirectly through the inhibitions it produces, such as Hamlet's reluctance to kill the man married to his mother. This, says Freud, illustrates 'the secular advance of repression' (1973–86, vol 4: 366). Such repression is the price for civilisation, and, as we shall see, it is a heavy price.

Lacan suggests that the move from the animism of our ancestors to modernity had to pass through monotheism. In the world of animism the supernatural 'rises up at every step, at the corner of every road, in grottoes, at crossroads'; its power 'cannot be overcome' (1992: 172) because it comes *from* everywhere. Only when gathered into the figure of a single God can the supernatural be confronted and dispersed.

Freud's commitment to scientific realism is utterly uncompromising. In one essay he analyses the records of a man in the seventeenth century who sold his soul to the devil, was possessed by demons but, through the good offices of the Virgin Mary, got his soul back again:

> The states of possession correspond to our neuroses, for the explanation of which we once more have recourse to psychical powers. In our eyes, the demons are bad and reprehensible wishes, derivatives of instinctual impulses that have been repudiated and repressed. We merely eliminate the projection of these mental entities into the external world which the Middle Ages carried out; instead, we regard them as having arisen in the patient's internal life, where they have their abode.
>
> (1973–86, vol 14: 383–84)

Of course that is not the end of the story. As Lacan remarks, after 'the death of God' (1992: 177), the supernatural God from out there lives on inside us.

Past and present

In 1913 in his book *Totem and Taboo* Freud attempts to give a historical – or strictly pre-historical – explanation of how human society first came into existence with the development of the Oedipus complex. Against the usual belief of sociology and history that the human exists essentially as it is within recent social and historical forms, Freud claims that there is a profound connection between ourselves and the earliest members of our species.

Freud begins by reviewing a wide number of tribal practices known to contemporary anthropology: a totem, which often takes the form of an animal, stands for the identity of the clan; the idea of 'taboo', which means both sacred and dangerously uncanny; belief in spirits, magic and the omnipotence of thoughts. In

Freud's analysis totemism has two basic laws – 'not to kill the totem animal and to avoid sexual intercourse with members of the totem clan of the opposite sex' (1973–86, vol 13: 85). But no one bothers to stop people doing something they don't *want* to do, so a prohibition only comes about in order to forbid a desire. The earliest people and ourselves are acting out of similar motives since the great prohibitions of totemism 'coincide in their content with the two crimes of Oedipus, who killed his father and married his mother' (ibid: 192).

It might have been better if Freud had left it there. Instead he goes on to explain the origin of human society *as such* by telling a story (202–5). Once upon a time humans (before they *were* human) lived in small groups ruled by a father who wanted all the women for himself. Not surprisingly, the young men got sick of this; one day they got together, killed the dominant male and ate him. They hated the father but since they also loved him they felt guilty. So they tried to revoke the deed by forbidding the killing of the father (the totem animal) and renouncing the women 'they desired and who had been their chief motive for despatching the father'. Human society, then, is founded 'on complicity in the common crime' (ibid: 208).

This story is Freud's own secular, sexy and violent version of the Garden of Eden. A major problem with it is that it presupposes what it is meant to explain. Aggression, desire and guilt are already *there* and lead to the events of the narrative when the narrative was really supposed to explain how these feelings came into existence.

Conventional social studies can be accused of unconsciously accepting rational behaviour as the norm for human society. Freud, in contrast, finds seemingly archaic attitudes alive and well in contemporary society – the taboos of so-called primitive people are 'not so remote from us' (ibid: 75) as we would like to think. Obsessional patients, for example, believe their thoughts alone can make things happen. If the inhabitants of New Caledonia have taboo feelings about certain animals, so did Little Hans (ibid:

189). Just as the life of the infant is continuous with the life of the adult, so the forms of drive developed in our ancestors remain with us even while the species has moved deeper into civilisation, human society and repression. What mainly distinguishes our species from the other animals is not reason but the unconscious: the incest taboo represented inside us by the Oedipus complex.

The taboo of virginity

Between 1910 and 1917 Freud wrote three essays as 'Contributions to the Psychology of Love'. The third of these, 'The Taboo of Virginity', offers striking evidence for the view that animist society has not simply vanished into modernity. Freud begins with anthropological material, noting that among people living in the oldest forms of human society virginity is not considered important but defloration is. In fact, charge attaches not just to the taking of virginity but to a whole range of what are seen as specifically feminine activities, such as menstruation, pregnancy, childbirth, so that one might conclude 'that women are altogether taboo' (1973–86, vol 7: 270). But to set up a taboo always shows a fear of danger; all the rules surrounding women express a 'generalised dread of women' (ibid: 271).

Freud proposes that this dread 'is based on the fact that woman is different from man, for ever incomprehensible and mysterious, strange and therefore apparently hostile' (ibid.). His phrasing does not criticise what it describes but it does make the situation crystal clear. Men assume masculinity is normal and right (and of course phallic) and therefore regard women as other, strange, 'different *from man*' (my italics). Men then project these fears about difference back onto the figure of woman as though she was responsible for them.

Freud does not subscribe to the flattering illusion that the oldest forms of human society are one thing and modern civilised life quite another. In men's 'dread of women' there is 'nothing which is not still alive among ourselves' (ibid.). An example can be found in the *Guardian* (29 June 1998). Under this headline, 'Now we're grown up – we can talk Tampax with tea', it was reported that commercial television in Britain was going to be allowed to transmit ads for 'sanitary protection' (sanpro) before 9.00pm (but not between 3.30 and 5.10pm, time set aside for children's television). However evasive – either as the 'It's my life' lycra-clad babe-on-rollerblades or featuring 'diagrams and phials of blue solutions' used to indicate blood, much of the 'British public is still sensitive about sanpro advertising'. In 1997 these advertisements had provoked 60 letters of complaint and in 1992, 333 letters, many of which focused on Claire Rayner's 'wings' ad for Vespre Silhouettes – 'Unique "Wings" for extra Protection'.

An agency representative was quoted as claiming, 'Most women are still very embarrassed or offended at having these messages beamed into their living rooms as they sit beside their husbands or boyfriends'. Despite the recent relaxation over timing, the words 'leakage' or 'odour' are still banned. From this contemporary expression of 'dread of women' one would hardly guess that just over half the population menstruate for most of their adult lives.

FREUD AND LENINISM

The idea that there is a deep continuity between the earliest members of our species and those living today also shapes Freud's view of contemporary political events. We have seen what Marxism thinks of psychoanalysis but it is not so widely known that Freud commented directly on Marxism and the Soviet Revolution. In the *New Introductory Lectures* of 1933 Freud endorses this as a 'tremendous experiment' (1973–86, vol 2: 218) on the grounds that it might 'put an end to the material need of the masses' as well as attend to 'the cultural demands of the individual' (ibid.). Freud has no difficulty with the materialist assertion that social life is ultimately determined by the economic base. His doubt is whether changing the economic base is sufficient to transform culture and ideology.

Since the child's super-ego is modelled on that of their parents, each subject becomes, Freud says, 'the vehicle of tradition':

> It seems likely that what are known as materialist views of history sin in underestimating this factor. They brush it aside with the remark that human 'ideologies' are nothing other than the product and superstructure of their contemporary economic conditions. That is true, but very probably not the whole truth. Mankind never lives entirely in the present. The past, the tradition of the race and of the people, lives on in the ideologies of the superego, and yields only slowly to the influences of the present and to new changes; and so long as it operates through the superego it plays a powerful part in human life, independently of economic conditions.
>
> (ibid: 99)

Freud accepts an idea of historical progress, though with the qualification that ideologies only yield to the influences of the present 'slowly'. However, he opens up another dimension behind such conceptions. Conventional historical thinking concentrates on the decade, century, period or even sometimes the epoch. Inside this historical time Freud sees *another* kind of time at work, the time of the species, linking contemporary life with the first humans of all. If there really are two kinds of time like this, it will be very difficult to reconcile usual social theories with the idea of the unconscious, to integrate Marx and Freud.

POSSIBLE RECONCILIATIONS?

I shall turn nevertheless to consider a number of attempts to bring historical theory into line with the idea of the unconscious, in each case assessing how far each gets in the direction of a full reconciliation of the two perspectives. It is not helpful to look for any such discussion in orthodox social studies because generally these pay little attention at all to psychoanalysis. Significantly, this is not the case with the Marxist tradition. Partly because it has a dedicated interest in theoretical questions, twentieth-century Marxism has tried seriously to take on board the challenge of Freud.

Frankfurt and Adorno

In 1933 Wilhelm Reich published *The Mass Psychology of Fascism*. Analysis of economic and political factors leading to the development of fascism was joined with an account of how repression in the petit-bourgeois family encouraged aggression and contributed to the rise of Hitler. During the 1930s the work of the Frankfurt school – Theodore Adorno, Max Horkheimer, Erich Fromm and Herbert Marcuse – also brought Freud's insights to discussion of political and cultural issues. Adorno's essay of 1941 on popular music is a good example.

In popular music, Adorno argued, 'every detail is substitutable' (1992: 213), 'the whole is pre-given and pre-accepted'. Such 'standardisation' divests the listener of 'spontaneity' and encourages '*standard reactions*' (ibid: 214). Each tune is just different enough to give the effect of 'pseudo-individualisation', so that 'cultural mass production' is endowed 'with the halo of free choice' (ibid: 217). The formal properties of popular music reveal its origin in capitalism and commodity production.

At the same time, as Adorno briskly admits, 'people want to have fun' (ibid: 219), to 'escape from the boredom of mechanised labour'. There is the 'poor shop girl' who 'identifies with Ginger Rogers'. He suggests that listeners to emotional music 'consume music in order to be allowed to weep' (ibid: 221):

> The actual function of sentimental music lies rather in the temporary release given to the awareness that one has missed fulfilment. . . . Emotional music has become the image of the mother who says, 'Come and weep, my child'.
>
> (ibid: 222)

This is as strange as it is striking, and perhaps means something like this: lost, along with the possibility of happiness, the mother is (impossibly) refound as she bids the child to weep for her loss. Similarly, the imaginary fullness of 'sentimental music' reinstates lack by insisting so coercively on the plenitude meant to displace the lack in the first place.

Adorno's analysis of popular music builds a bridge outward from the social formation towards subjectivity though it is open to the criticism that what is being referred to is not really subjectivity at all since it is determined essentially as an *effect* of the social. Then he leaps across to the other side and gives a suggestive, psychoanalytic account of popular music but an account which assumes an active *autonomy* in the operation of the unconscious beyond any clear social determination ('people want to have fun'). A gap remains between Adorno's Marxism and his psychoanalysis.

Althusser

In 1964 the French Marxist philosopher, Louis Althusser, published an essay on 'Freud and Lacan' (1977: 181–202) welcoming psychoanalysis as a materialist account of the construction of the subject. In a later essay, 'Ideology and Ideological State Apparatuses' (ibid: 121–73), written after the 'events' of May 1968 in France, Althusser aims to draw together the relation between ideology and the unconscious. Through the concept of *interpellation*, adapted from Lacan's analysis of the ego in 'The Mirror Stage', he wants to explain how we are constructed by society to see our social world as so natural and obvious we would not want to change it.

Ideology takes babies and turns them into speaking subjects who have a place in society; ideology works on people so that they think of themselves as *free* individuals. Althusser's model for this effect is a voice which demands imperiously, 'Who's there?', and I reply submissively, 'It is me'. Through this 'hailing' or inter-pellation I come to recognise myself in an 'Absolute, *Other Subject*, i.e. God' (ibid: 166). My sense of my own freedom results from this hailing – in this process ideology hides itself, enabling subjects to experience their own produced identity as neutral and self-evidently *there*.

Some questions will indicate cracks in this welding together of two kinds of theory. First, Althusser supposes that identity comes about primarily in response to an imperative – I am hailed by the superego and the norms of society rather than, as Lacan says, drawn into identity through fantasy. Then there is the problem that an 'I' which can *recognise* itself in the Other Subject is an ego which is already *given*, able to perform the tasks of recognising (see Hirst 1979). Third, Althusser's notion of ideology simply cannot go wrong, it cannot fail to interpellate a subject into a perfect and invisible fit with the role society has ready for it. That is not how the unconscious works, however, since any effect of unified identity is fragile, provisional and unstable. Society does in a general sense interpellate subjects but they always feel resentment or resistance to the process. If they did not there might be no possibility of social change at all.

Jameson

Fredric Jameson in *The Political Unconscious* (1981) conceives history and specifically the Marxist idea of class struggle as an 'absent cause' (ibid: 35), the Real. This exists outside signification and can only be encountered in forms of narrative, a view which is clearly analogous to Lacan's account of the real and the symbolic. Of the various narratives on offer, such as the Christian narrative for example, Marxism is, so Jameson asserts, the most comprehensive and persuasive, the best possible interpretation.

Marx certainly assumes that we take up class positions involuntarily, not as an act of free choice. However, quite apart from the question of what is left of Marxism if it becomes merely the greatest story ever told, it is some stretch to suppose that awareness of class is *repressed* in the same kind of dynamic by which consciousness comes about only because the unconscious is repressed. Though he has drawn brilliantly on psychoanalysis as a model or paradigm for his theorisation, Jameson's 'political unconscious' is simply not unconscious.

Žižek

Since Althusser, Slavoj Žižek has given completely new impetus to the relation between Marxism and the unconscious in a series of stunning performances, starting with *The Sublime Object of Ideology* (1989). Whereas others have *begun* with Marxism and attempted to incorporate psychoanalysis into it, Žižek starts with subjectivity and then moves out towards the social.

For Žižek ideology is not something we consciously think but rather something we unconsciously practise – when we behave '*as if* the President incarnates the Will of the people, *as if* the Party expresses the objective interests of the working class' (1989: 36). What Žižek terms '*ideological fantasy*' consists in overlooking 'the illusion which is structuring our real, effective relationship to reality' (ibid: 32–33). After referring to Lacan's discussion of the dream, 'Father, don't you see I'm burning?', Žižek says '"Reality" is a fantasy-construction which enables us to mask the real of our desire' and 'it is exactly the same with ideology' (ibid: 45). The real goal of ideology is '*the consistency of the ideological attitude itself*' (ibid: 84); via ideology '*pure difference is perceived as Identity*' (ibid: 99); '"Let the facts speak for themselves" is perhaps the archstatement of ideology' (1994: 11).

Misrecognition, identity, consistency, the self-evident: in Lacan these are all effects of the imaginary – what masks through fantasy the real and the symbolic, conferring the effect of stability on the ego. Žižek's 'ideology' is essentially the Lacanian imaginary.

This is very suggestive. But if I refer to an example, the question of whether it integrates Marxism and psychoanalysis will more or less answer itself:

> the sinking of the *Titanic* had a traumatic effect, it was a shock, 'the impossible happened'; the unsinkable ship had sunk; but the point is that precisely as a shock, this sinking arrived at its proper time – 'the time was waiting for it': even before it actually happened there was a place opened, reserved for it in fantasy-space. It had such a terrific impact on 'social imaginary' [*sic*] by virtue of the fact that it was expected.
>
> (1989: 69)

Žižek notes that a novel of 1898 even foretold such an event. Transatlantic liners were 'floating palaces, wonders of technical progress', 'the meeting-place of the cream of society' (ibid: 70). What sunk was a symbol of society 'as a stable totality with well-defined class distinctions', a 'barbaric' accident which represented 'the approaching catastrophe of European civilisation itself' (ibid.). It is not the case, then, that something happened and people responded but that the 'social imaginary' was already in place and seized on the event.

This account raises an important issue. To whom is this 'fantasy-space' or 'social imaginary' present and who experiences the sinking of the *Titanic* as a symptom? It can only be some collective Western subject living around 1912. But that is the not what the unconscious is like in either Freud or Lacan, for whom desire, like the dream, is your own rather than collective. A second question we need to pose is: who resists this fantasy? For there is little question here of a partial or uneven identification. Like Althusser's interpellation, Žižek's 'social imaginary' works for everyone. This theory is very interesting but one has to ask whether it is really a theory of the unconscious as understood by Freud and Lacan.

Žižek is such a skilful player you have got to keep your eye on the ball and ignore his fancy foot-work. No doubt the Victorian *fin de siècle* was taken up by people in all kinds of fantasies (melancholia, neurotic anxiety, death wish etc.). But we should not miss how Žižek runs together the operation of fantasy with a specifically *social* content, ideology in the sense of meaning shaped in relations of social power. The 'floating palaces' do figure as fantasy objects but their meaning as 'stable totality with well-defined class distinctions' is something else altogether. However plausible and persuasive Žižek's analysis, fantasy and social meaning, the unconscious and ideology, are *superimposed*, not unified.

Freud and Malinowski

A chapter by Paul Q. Hirst and Penny Woolley (1982: 140–63) contains one of the most sustained attempts to assess an account of the same object of inquiry from both a sociological and a psychoanalytic perspective. They set out to read Freud's analysis of the incest taboo from *Totem and Taboo* against the classic anthropological study of Trobriand Island society by Bronislaw Malinowski in *Sex and Repression in Savage Society* (1937).

Freud assumes that the unconscious is 'universal in its basic contents and mechanisms' (Hirst and Woolley 1982: 150), that a Viennese member of the liberal professions and an Australian aboriginal are linked by 'similar mechanisms of unconscious thought' (ibid: 151). Freud is not concerned 'to explain institutions in the way a sociologist or anthropologist would', rather 'he derives religion, law, and custom directly from the dynamic of the psyche' (ibid: 152) as though states of mind gave rise directly to institutions.

Malinowski argues that the family structure of Polynesian

culture is radically different from what is supposed in Freud's discussion of the Oedipus complex. Descent is reckoned through the female line; the son inherits from his maternal uncle, and he, not the father, is an authority figure (the father is a nurse and playmate). Yet the child does not come into sexual conflict with this uncle. Paternity and sexuality are strongly related in Trobriand Island society and a son is forbidden members of his uncle's clan and especially his sister. Sexual conflict here is centred on the relation between brother and sister rather than between parent and child. Against Freud, Malinowski can argue 'the building up of the sentiments, the conflicts which this implies, depend largely upon the sociological mechanism which works in a given society' (ibid: 155).

Malinowski treats sexuality as inherently genital and deriving from the body, dismissing Freud's concept of the unconscious as 'metaphysical' (ibid.). He has no account of the libidinal attachments at work in families and groups. While Freud's attempt to explain institutions exclusively in terms of unconscious feelings is inadequate, so is Malinowski's willingness to ignore them altogether: 'if Freud makes social relations the unmediated results of psychic states, Malinowski makes social relations, in the last instance, patterns of culture' (ibid: 156).

Sociological explanation and the concept of the unconscious do not refute each other, they simply are not in competition. The two human sciences, psychoanalysis and sociology, are incommensurate, and engaged in analysis of different objects. Nevertheless, as Hirst and Woolley conclude, 'the psychic-symbolic domain interpenetrates with culture and social relations' (ibid: 159).

So there is always an unconscious 'inside' informing and supporting social phenomena. At this point what we need is a good metaphor. Stephen Heath provides it by borrowing from Saussure: the two processes of historical society and the unconscious form a 'necessary simultaneity – like the recto and verso [front and back] of a piece of paper' (1976: 62).

It is only in rare instances that an unconscious effect, through its excess, forces itself on attention: attacks on women wearing fur, Methodism in the late eighteenth-century, the 'Final Solution' (both these two examples are still to come). Usually, an unconscious effect is not so obvious. We need to be clear what is at stake here. If social meaning and unconscious meaning occur *simultaneously* but cannot be measured against each other, then it will always be open for someone from the social sciences to pull out the social feature in a phenomenon, claim that is all that counts, and ignore the rest. Of course a similar manoeuvre is possible for an advocate of psychoanalysis, who may claim that any social phenomena can be explained as an expression of the unconscious.

LACAN AND HISTORY

These attempts by Adorno, Althusser and the others to integrate Marx and Freud tend to confirm Freud's belief that there is no continuity between historical time and the time of the unconscious, that is, the time of the human species as a whole. As we turn now specifically to Lacan, we might expect his conception that subjectivity is produced within language and the symbolic order to point towards some combination of history and the unconscious. Surely Lacan will consolidate his analysis of the-subject-in-discourse by contrasting the modern, post-Renaissance subject with older versions of subjectivity – under feudalism, for example, or in ancient Greek society, for which the tragedies furnish plenty of evidence? Lacan, however, is scrupulous to concern himself only with the modern age. When he does discuss Sophocles' play *Antigone* he reads it not primarily in historical terms but as a justification for the view that, like Antigone in her determination to bury her brother, we should not yield in our desire (see 1992).

As his frequent references to Descartes and Pascal make clear, for Lacan 'the *moi*, the ego, of modern man' (1977a: 70) began to come into existence at the Renaissance. Descartes founded the modern subject in its capacity to doubt itself but for Lacan this reflective self-consciousness constitutes a deceptive version of the ego ideal: 'the philosophical *cogito* is at the centre of the mirage that renders modern man so sure of being himself even in his uncertainties about himself, and even in the mistrust he has learned to practise against the traps of self-love' (ibid: 165). Misrecognition occurs precisely in the scepticism the modern ego has learned to direct against itself.

In an essay of 1948 entitled 'Aggressivity' and written when things in Europe looked pretty bad, Lacan sounds a note of deep cultural pessimism. The modern ego, trusting in its own fantasies of autonomy and mastery as intensified 'by the barbarism of the Darwinian century' (ibid: 26), will win through to new levels of competitiveness, aggression, and desire for domination. In its egotism and self-deception it is gripped by what Lacan terms a 'modern neurosis' (ibid: 25).

At the end of the essay Lacan writes a fierce paragraph denouncing the decay of a traditional society, 'the increasing absence of all those saturations of the superego and ego ideal that are realised . . . in traditional societies', forms that extend from the rituals of everyday to 'the periodical festivals in which the community manifests itself'. Instead 'the promotion of the ego today culminates . . . in an ever more advanced realisation of man as individual' (ibid: 26–27).

How much weight should we give to Lacan's sombre rhetoric? One might take it more seriously if Lacan had explored some of the limitations of a traditional society such as the relatively closed world of the Middle Ages. But he refuses to imagine subjectivity outside the modern period. The reason for this is significant.

PSYCHOANALYSIS RELATIVE TO HISTORY

Lacan attacks psychoanalysts who believe they have 'access to a reality transcending aspects of history' (Lacan actually writes 'accès à une réalité transcendante aux aspects de l'histoire' – what appears at the top of page 120 in 1977a, 'access to a transcendent reality possessing the characteristics of history', is, alas, a complete mistranslation). Instead he stresses that the concepts and theoretical framework of psychoanalysis are relative to the modern period and the modern ego. The Oedipus complex 'occupies a privileged position, in the present state of Western civilisation' (1988a: 198) but could not appear in human history until matriarchy gave way to patriarchy.

In a passage which Dylan Evans has drawn attention to (see 1996) Lacan says that Socrates may have thought of something as the centre of his being but 'it is probably not made like the ego, which starts . . . towards the middle of the sixteenth, beginning of the seventeenth centuries' (1988b: 7). 'It is very difficult for us to imagine' that the modern psychology of the ego 'isn't eternal' (ibid: 6); it is very important to recognise that it is not.

Lacan is anxious to resist the gratifying idea that nothing ever really changes: when something comes to light 'which we are forced to consider as new . . . , well then, it creates its own perspective within the past, and we say – *This can never not have been there, this has existed from the beginning*' (ibid: 5). Since we are within language, for example, we cannot picture a time before there was language. We can only think about the unconscious *within* the categories of thought history has provided: the modern ego is the matrix for psychoanalysis. This conviction corresponds to Lacan's view that 'no metalanguage can be spoken' and 'there is no Other of the Other' (1977a: 311), no universal truth, that is, outside a given symbolic order. It contrasts with Freud's lofty belief in science.

THE UNCONSCIOUS AND HISTORY

LACAN ON VISION

So Lacan will commit himself only to the analysis of the modern ego within theoretical frameworks avowedly derived from the modern period. On this basis he constructs a brilliant account of the development of perspective in painting (1977b: 65–119), the representation of three dimensions in two worked out in Italy by Giotto, Masaccio, da Vinci and others especially in the fifteenth century (what the Italians call the 'Four Hundred' or Quattrocento). Lacan's discussion does so well in bringing together history and the unconscious that it suggests I should qualify my earlier claims that the two cannot be integrated. Well, in fact they are not actually *integrated* but since Lacan concentrates on the signifier, on textuality, they can be seen to operate in a simultaneity, together and in a manifest relation to each other. The same text opens onto ideological meaning as well as inviting a fantasy response (I have tried to develop this view elsewhere in relation to poetry, see Easthope 1989).

The detail of Lacan's argument is complicated and needs to be taken slowly. He begins with the story of being out with some fishermen when a small boy with them pointed to a sardine tin on the surface, glittering in the sun. He said, '*You see that can? Do you see it? Well, it doesn't see you*' (1977b: 95). No, it doesn't see you. But *someone* there might see you, since whatever I can see constitutes a point from which I could *be seen*. Lacan says 'That which is light looks at me' (ibid: 96) meaning that if there is light, I can see but can also be seen. I think I see the sardine tin. But the same light is the condition for someone else to look at me from there, a point of view I myself can never see from since it belongs to the Other

'I see only from one point, but in my existence I am looked at from all sides' (ibid: 72): to 'see the world' comes within the dominion of the conscious I. To 'be the object of the gaze' represents the operation of the unconscious, the domain of the Other on which I depend but which I can never lay claim to.

The history of Quattrocento painting shows that the aim has been for the look to overcome the gaze in a *dompte-regard*, 'a taming of the gaze' (ibid: 109). Perspective seeks to ensure that I see the represented image while the possibility of the gaze, *looking back*, is controlled and effaced. Painting techniques render the image as an *object* for my eye so trying to exclude the gaze of another.

Lacan gives a close analysis of the Quattrocento tradition, obviously ideological in that it promotes the new Renaissance ideal of 'the sovereign individual'. At the same time he explains how such vision always occasions desire. I desire to possess the image and what it represents but can only do so by looking. But looking presupposes the gaze of the Other, which is a prior condition for my look and within which I appear as an object. In this respect, the gaze of the Other provokes my desire since, as Lacan argues, desire is of the Other (see above, pp. 94–97). What I want to see but never can is how I look in the eyes of the Other. That gaze has a function as *objet petit a*, causing my desire while making it impossible to fulfil.

Quattrocento representation became the groundwork of conventional photography after around 1900, followed by 'moving pictures'. During the 1970s the English film journal, *Screen*, adapted Lacan's theory of vision to a critique of mainstream cinematic realism; it produced a position of visual dominance for the viewer but tried to conceal ways that position itself was produced, through lighting, camera movement, editing and narrative (see Heath 1981). Lacan's inquiry has also become widely influential in art theory, for example, providing Norman Bryson with a means to criticise the Quattrocento effect of realism without relying on the idea of art as reflection of reality (see 1983).

THE UNCONSCIOUS IN GROUPS AND EVENTS

There is a qualitative move in turning from an account of texts to other social phenomena. Consisting of signifiers, texts open simultaneously onto disjunct kinds of meaning, fantasy and ideological meaning. By contrast, for institutions, social groups, political events, the analysis has to be more complicated. Nevertheless, the unconscious is fully active in all of these. I shall consider three examples: group identity, a constitutional document, the utopian tradition.

Group identification

All effective human groups are glued together by strong identification. It is surprising that writers on history pay so little attention to this. In his magisterial work, *The Making of the English Working Class*, Edward Thompson is happy to draw on ideas of sexual repression, displacement and what he calls '"womb-regressive" imagery' (1968: 408) when talking about something manifestly irrational such as the excesses of evangelical religion at the turn of the nineteenth century. His main thesis is that 'In the years between 1780 and 1832 most English working people came to feel an identity of interests as between themselves and as against their rulers and employers' (ibid: 12). It does not occur to him that here in this feeling of identity (though in less spectacular form) an unconscious process may be at work.

In *Group Psychology and the Analysis of the Ego* Freud begins by noting that collective identity is precisely that, a group identity defined over against what differs from it. Even friends show some hostility to each other but in the group intolerance vanishes: individuals 'behave as though they were uniform, tolerate the peculiarities of its other members' (1973–86, vol 11: 131–32). It is as though the group is in possession of 'a sort of collective mind' (ibid: 99).

To explain the 'love instincts' (ibid: 120) that make groups adhere, Freud puts forward an argument of elegant simplicity. Groups – *all* groups – work through narcissism: members identify with the same object and therefore identify with each other. They '*have put one and the same object in the place of their ego ideal*' and have '*consequently identified themselves with one another in their ego*' (ibid: 147). It is what would happen if a lot of people were in love with the same person, such as Princess Di, for instance, or Leonardo DiCaprio.

This common object may be a person, such as the General in an army or Jesus in the Christian church (Freud's own examples). But it need not be a person at all since 'an idea, an abstraction' will do just as well and may be the sign of a more advanced culture (ibid: 129). In a football team players share identification with the manager but also with the *idea* of the team's success. In a nation individuals may identify with 'the Constitution', 'the principles of 1789', or simply a conglomeration of images and ideas marked out as peculiar to the nation: for example, landscape, 'fair play', cuisine, discipline, a sense of humour.

Does Freud's account of groups really need illustration? In a whole series of classic American war films, from *Sands of Iwo Jima* (1949) to *The Naked and the Dead* (1958), *The Dirty Dozen* (1967) and *Big Red One* (1980) down to *Saving Private Ryan* (1998) we see a bunch of disparate individuals forged into a unified command by a tough sergeant. But if this analysis of groups is persuasive, we need be careful. Psychoanalysis would suggest that the very thing which pulls a group together can turn as easily to pulling another group apart. This is exactly what happens in *Sands of Iwo Jima* and the others, where the new-found unity of the platoon or battalion is marked out and confirmed by violent aggression against comparable groups of 'the enemy'.

For psychoanalysis, all societies, groups and institutions are informed by the basic structuring of unconscious forces discussed in *Totem and Taboo* and *Group Psychology*. Besides these, however, all kinds of local conjunctures and historical experiences will mobilise particular effects, though these are variable and open to debate. Fairly obviously, for example, when a country declares war aggressive feelings are going to be excited.

The American Declaration of Independence

> When in the course of human events, it becomes necessary for one people to dissolve the political bands which have connected them with another, and to assume among the powers of the earth, the separate and equal station to which the Laws of Nature and of Nature's God entitle them, a decent respect to the opinions of mankind requires that they should declare the causes which impel them to the separation.
>
> We hold these truths to be self-evident, that all men are created equal, that they are endowed by their Creator with certain unalienable rights, that among these are life, liberty and the pursuit of happiness. That to secure these rights, governments are instituted among men, deriving their just powers from the consent of the governed. That whenever any form of government becomes destructive of these ends, it is the right of the people to alter and abolish it, and to institute new government . . .

This may appear a set of perfectly self-conscious, rational propositions. In fact the opening passage of the American Declaration sings a hymn to the unconscious pleasures of narcissism, the 'drive to mastery' and the (supposedly) autonomous ego. It specifically denies that human groups are united by emotional or libidinal ties; 'bands' connecting peoples are 'political' and it becomes necessary to dissolve them if governments do not derive their sovereignty from 'the consent of the governed'. If a government does not do this 'it is the right of the people to alter it'. All any other people deserve is 'decent respect' for their 'opinions' and an explanation of reasons.

Nature (and Nature's rather subdued deity) ensure that individuals are equal, self-sufficient and independent, as though we all leapt into the world fully-formed like Gargantua who, in the early Renaissance text by Rabelais, shouted 'Some drink, some drink' the moment he was born. They make self-conscious decisions by giving consent to governments, or withholding it. Each has a right to 'life, liberty and the pursuit of happiness', which leaves open the question of the life and happiness of other members of the group. Truth is known to each person empirically, from experience, for it is 'self-evident' (*held* to be self-evident). Just as 'a people' is said to be 'separate and equal', so also are these individuals, who in aggregate add up to a society.

Moreover, and perhaps surprisingly, women should not dream of claiming these rights themselves, unless the term 'men' covers both sexes. If it does not, then narcissism is bound up with the homoerotic interests of the male bond, just as it so often is in a classic Western movie. And we have to remember that in 1776 slaves were not really considered to be 'men'.

I do not want to be misunderstood. I am resolutely in favour of rights and democracy. And the Declaration of 1776 is much more committed to the sovereignty of the people than the Constitution of 1787, which weakens popular sovereignty by breaking it up between Congress, the Presidency, the Supreme Court and the separate States, each of which seems designed to cancel the others out (see Lazare 1998). But to view people as no more than separate, self-sufficient, self-conscious individuals and to generalise this as the principle of a whole society gives a very partial account of what people – and groups – are like.

In a way I have made the example easy for myself by choosing a text. Events around the conjuncture of 1776 really need to be considered more widely to see how different subjects identified themselves unevenly in the words of the Declaration. Many supported it but not all of them.

The founding of the United States is certainly steeped in utopian belief, that a 'new man' has arisen in a 'New World', free at last from Europe (the castrating father). But the first Americans – white, male Americans – had had such a bad time under the corrupt authoritarianism of George III that they wrote into the legislation all kinds of rights of dissent, including after 1791 the right to 'freedom of speech' as well as the right to carry guns. I shall pursue the possibility that utopian social belief has a strong unconscious component by looking at the tradition as it develops from the French Revolution and on into the Soviet Revolution.

The utopian tradition

Besides Nazism and the 'Final Solution' the major question of our times is how the utopian vision of Marxism could ever lead to the atrocities of Stalin's Soviet Union, in which over 20 million Russians were exterminated in the camps of the Gulag? The idea of the unconscious would suggest that an answer lies in the way utopian idealism is underpinned by the ego ideal. By this I mean the 'ego ideal' not in Freud's sense – what anticipates the superego – but rather in Lacan's definition of it as seeing yourself with others in the way you like to be seen (see above, pp. 62–65). Utopian idealism can be traced back to the French Revolution.

On 27 August 1789 France adopted the Declaration of the Rights of Man and Citizen. So far so good, but the Revolution went on to believe that a permanent change had come over human nature. The German philosopher Friedrich Hegel acclaimed the Revolution as uniting, for the first time in history, principles of rationality with the practice of a liberal constitution: 'Never since the sun had stood in the firmament and the planets revolved around him [*sic*] had it been perceived that man's existence centres in his head, *i.e.* in Thought, inspired by which he builds up the world of reality' (1956: 447).

The French leaders agreed and signalled the new birth by renaming 1792 'Year 1' of a new epoch and dispensing with the old Roman names for months in favour of more exact meteorological terms drawn from the natural world ('Thermidor', 'hot'; 'Brumaire', 'misty'). The Goddess of Reason was solemnly installed in the cathedral of Notre Dame. At the Festival of the Unity and

Indivisibility of the Republic held on 10 August 1793 'the Fountain of Regeneration', a huge statue of a woman with water pouring freely from her breasts, was put up on the site of the Bastille. Wordsworth welcomed the Revolution as 'Human nature seeming born again' (1979, Book VI, l: 341).

The problem was that this vision of unity, homogeneity and rational perfection did not allow for dissent and reasoned disagreement. The guillotine was introduced in March 1792. Aristocrats and other miscreants were followed to the scaffold by a procession of revolutionary leaders who made the mistake of being outvoted or voicing unpopular opinions. Each was hauled before the Committee of Public Safety, condemned by a Revolutionary Tribunal and decapitated. 1789 seems to be the first time when totalitarian institutions were given public-service names.

Unfortunately, in working out conditions for the Communist Revolution, Marx looked back to the utopianism of France. As the first sentence of the Communist Manifesto states, 'the history of hitherto-existing society is the history of class struggles' (Marx and Engels 1950, 1: 33). Class struggle is caused by the exploitation of one class by another. Under capitalism the working class is alienated from the fruits of its labour and true human possibilities because capital and factories are privately owned by a class that keeps all the power and fruits of labour for themselves. The solution seemed to be: eradicate capitalism, organise the working class *as* the ruling class through a political party, expropriate the expropriators – and it will all come right. According to this logic, 'pre-history' will end as class antagonism becomes automatically superseded in the birth of a harmonious and conflict-free utopia.

What Marx omitted from this account was a place for democratic argument, democratic opposition. Perhaps it was not his fault but when Lenin and the others took power in 1917 this is the model they followed. Any sign of dissent rapidly came to be judged as betraying the ideals of the Revolution, ideals people were supposed to express constantly in the way they behaved for each other. For example, a woman took down the portrait of Stalin for spring-cleaning and was immediately condemned. It is said that the 'Purges' (another significant euphemism) of the 1930s only ground to a halt, temporarily, because those accused of treason and spying were actually a *majority* in the population.

Even Nazism calls on a twisted form of utopianism with its belief that it had founded a new order, a 'Thousand Year Reich' based on bizarre ideas of pagan revival and racial purity. In making these remarks I am not arguing that the ego ideal in the sense Lacan used the term is all bad or that we could ever manage entirely without it in some form. And clearly other factors come into play; both France in 1789 and Russia in 1917 already had fiercely authoritarian traditions. But it is certainly likely that utopianism works powerfully to promote the ego ideal and is in turn supported by it.

This need not involve society at large. A recent press report, 'Communal hell of the wild child in hippie utopia' (*Sunday Times*, 30 August 1998), reported the experiences of someone brought up in a commune. He says:

> The worst thing about commune life was the total lack of recognition for the internal power struggles that are inherent in any group. This led to the effective creation of a hierarchy governed by fear and violence.

Men were on top and spent all day pretending to fix old tractors in the workshop 'where they drank tea and smoked roll-ups'. The women 'were the workhorses' and the only ones who looked after the children. Bathed in the fantasy of its own unity and perfection, the ego ideal makes it very hard for a utopian group to encourage dissent as right and necessary.

HAPPINESS AND HUMAN NATURE

During the 1960s a generation grew up imagining there was no heaven but that if you really followed your desires – *really* followed them – you would find full happiness, without repression. I have to admit that like many others at that time I thought so too. Freud is uncompromising: 'belief in the "goodness" of human nature is one of those evil illusions by which mankind expect their lives to be beautified and made easier while in reality they only cause damage' (1973–86, vol 2: 137). 'A re-ordering of human relations' which would introduce a 'golden age' by removing 'the sources of dissatisfaction with civilisation by renouncing . . . the suppression of instincts' (1973–86, vol 12: 185) just cannot happen.

Freud gives three reasons in the main why we can never be really happy. The first reason for the lack of complete satisfaction is the Oedipus complex. All human society is founded 'on complicity in the common crime' (1973–86, vol 13: 208), in a profound and irresolvable tension between desire for the mother and prohibition on the mother, between desire to kill the father and prohibition on killing the father. What binds the group together originates in fierce denial of forces that would tear it apart.

A second source of human unhappiness is the super-ego. Civilisation is only brought about by marshalling for itself energies *greater* than those of the original aggression: because conscience can turn against the individual 'the same harsh aggressiveness' they originally felt (1973–86, vol 12: 315). The species is always trapped in an internal war between instinct and renunciation, drive and the super-ego. Civilisation is not a harmonious, once-and-for-all achievement: it is the *continuing* effect of the repression of violence.

A third source is the death drive. As Freud says in *The Ego and the Id*, the super-ego 'rages against the ego with merciless violence' (1973–86, vol 11: 394) until it becomes 'a pure culture of the death instinct (drive)' (ibid.). In Freud's mature view, Eros, the life drive, is opposed to Thanatos, the death drive. We like to think that we are inside the circle of life and death is something outside. Freud believes 'there is life as well as death', that death is part of life for 'the two are mingled in the process of living' (1973–86, vol 2: 141). Thanatos and aggression can enter every aspect of human behaviour.

LACAN AND AGGRESSION

Lacan takes a different view of the origins of human violence and cruelty. As one might expect, he finds it rooted in the ego. Individual identity comes about by being borrowed from the Other. The subject aspires to homogeneity and permanence, identifying its unity (above all) in an image of the body as a unified whole and fearing (above all) a corresponding image of the body in pieces (through 'images of castration, mutilation, dismember-ment, dislocation, evisceration, devouring, bursting open of the body', 1977a: 11).

'It is', Lacan asserts in his essay on 'Aggressivity' (1948), 'in this erotic relation, in which the human individual fixes upon himself an image that alienates him from himself, that are to be found the energy and the form on which this organisation of the passions that he will call his ego is based' (1977a: 19). Since the ego was never *there* in the first place it has to be organised out of fragments bound together into a temporary unity. The active force that holds it together is always likely to be released against anything that threatens to pull it to pieces. The ego and feelings of aggression are born together. In fact, aggression is 'the correlative tendency of a mode of identification that we call narcissistic' (ibid: 16).

Everything that is not the 'I' endangers the 'I'. Flux challenges its permanence, spatial difference its fixity, any alterity its identity, any outside its inside. I try to preserve my coherence by denying what undermines it and projecting internal threats onto the outside. Developing in a 'paranoiac structure' the ego throws 'back on to the world the disorder' from which it is composed (ibid: 20). Human beings, it has to be remembered, are the only species who will take members of their own species to bits just for fun. At worst the logic of aggression deriving from the ego must be, 'If I'm taking you to pieces, nothing can be taking me to pieces'.

What is the case for individual identity must hold for collective identity. Groups identify themselves by denying the other, enforcing a boundary between inside and outside, 'us' and 'them'. Collective identification with *my* people depends on the possibility of expelling – violently if necessary – anyone who is not one of *my* people. The conclusion of a theory of the unconscious is that this is a possibility human beings can never finally be rid of.

7

CONCLUSION: GIVING IT ALL AWAY

After the Museum of Fine Arts was opened in Vienna in 1889, Freud was a frequent visitor. At the top of the grand staircase in the magnificent entrance there is a huge statue by Canova of Theseus killing a centaur. It symbolises civilisation vanquishing barbarism, though it is significant that it has to depend on the methods of barbarism to do so. At that time people could still believe in the goodness of human nature, that culture and science were spreading inevitably outward from a European centre across the world.

Today, on the edge of a new millennium, we are differently placed. Our century has witnessed: the killing fields of Verdun and Passchendaele; the Nazi–Soviet war of 1941–45 in which 'the total war dead of the Soviet Union' was 27 million, 9 million soldiers and 18 million civilians (Beevor 1998: 428), and in which prisoners were not taken – often those captured were stuffed into oil drums, doused with petrol and set alight; the 'Final Solution'; the carpet bombing of Germany by the British and American air forces, killing over 600,000 women and children: 60,000 in three nights at Hamburg, 35,000 in a 12-hour period at Dresden; the firestorm bombing of Tokyo on 10 March 1945 which killed over 120,000 people, more than either atomic bomb dropped on Hiroshima and Nagasaki. In the past 10 years there has been genocide of a million people in Rwanda, as well as 'ethnic cleansing' in former Yugoslavia. As the song says, 'there's nothing you can do that can't be done'.

In 1995 I gave some lectures at the University of Silesia in Katowice. As part of the visit I was taken to nearby Oswiecim, the Polish name for Auschwitz. Walking round Birkenau, the second camp, a man came up to me in tears and said simply, 'How could this happen?'. Dutifully I rehearsed the historical arguments: the humiliation of Germany's defeat in the First World War, the Treaty of Versailles which made Germany politically independent but stopped it being economically viable, the incredible inflation crisis in the early 1920s and then, in 1929, the collapse of the world economy, thousands out of work, severe depression. In the election of 1928 the Nazi party had won less than three per cent of the vote but in the extraordinary circumstances of 1933 Hitler became Chancellor, although hardly any Germans had any real idea of what he had in mind. After I finished, standing where we were, I saw it meant almost nothing. What we were trying to think about went far beyond any rational explanation in terms of historical cause and effect.

A traditional humanism had tried to separate what people do into an inside and an outside, to mark off civilisation from barbarism, human and inhuman, Theseus and the centaur. Against this view psychoanalysis demands humility, which means that we have to take human and inhuman together, as equal possibilities.

Psychoanalysis therefore relieves us of the burden of believing that our species is better than we know. Such pessimism – or realism – discourages the seductive dangers of utopian thinking. It is absolutely democratic insofar as no-one's unconscious is better than anyone else's.

Though contradictory, the unconscious has its own invincible logic (see Borch-Jacobsen 1990); Freud cites a boy of 10 who said after his father's sudden death, 'I know father's dead but what I can't understand is why he doesn't come home to supper' (1973–86, vol 4: 355 fn.). While resisting full-blown scientific rationalism the theory of the unconscious does not surrender to the impressionism of common sense. It does not simply describe but seeks to *analyse* and *explain* what people do, restating private experience in public language. Freud trusted that he could create a science of the unconscious; he never wavered in his passionate belief in civilisation, in science as one of its highest achievements.

Lacan rejects any faith in truth as an absolute or a foundation of knowledge outside human practice; there is, he says, 'no Other of the Other' (1977a: 311). Yet Lacan insists that his own analysis is repeatable, teachable. He never stopped looking for forms of rational explanation to formalise his insights even knowing how limited and partial they must be. This ambivalence seems evident in his attempt to create a single diagram of the whole truth about the psyche (see the 'Completed Graph', 1977a: 315). So if psychoanalysis is pessimistic, it is a *lucid* pessimism.

I have followed in the steps of this Enlightenment tradition by trying to write a short and clear book 'about' the unconscious. But this endeavour is necessarily a betrayal. Anything which claims to 'know' or 'discuss' the unconscious disregards the nature and process of the unconscious itself.

The unconscious is *beyond*. Its activity exceeds any statement, any explanation.

At the Renaissance Descartes founded the tradition which made consciousness and the ego the centre of human subjectivity and being – '*I think, therefore I am*' (1960: 24). Since then, as Freud says in 'A Difficulty in the Path of Psycho-Analysis'(1953–74, vol 17: 136–44), our 'universal narcissism' has suffered 'from the researches of science'. A first blow was discovering the earth was not the centre of the universe, a second when Darwin proved that ours is just another species, 'more closely related to some' and 'more distant to others'. The third blow to Western self-love came when psychoanalysis showed 'that *the ego is not master in its own house*'.

To be sure of the existence of the unconscious all you need to do is think of the acts of your own mental life 'as if they belonged to someone else' (1973–86, vol 11: 171). Freud's conclusion is that 'we must learn to emancipate ourselves from the importance of the symptom of "being conscious"' (ibid: 197). Lacan openly attacks Descartes' notion of the priority of the ego. The idea of a split between conscious and unconscious forces us to reverse Descartes' position. Instead, Lacan offers, 'I think where I am not, therefore I am where I do not think' (1977a: 166). Whether I want it or not my unconscious will follow its own rules and do its own thinking for me.

This insight is confirmed – and anticipated – by the great international artistic and cultural movement that swept Europe and the United States between 1900 and 1930: Modernism. In 1916 Ezra Pound wrote:

> In the 'search for oneself', in the search for 'sincere self-expression', one gropes, one finds some seeming verity. One says 'I am' this, that or the other, and with the words scarcely uttered one ceases to be that thing.
>
> (1960: 85)

Eliot in his famous essay on 'Tradition and the Individual Talent' (1919) declared that 'the point of view which I am struggling to attack is perhaps related to the metaphysical theory of the substantial unity of the soul' (1966: 19). In an interview of 1926 Bertolt Brecht said:

> The continuity of the ego is a myth. A man is an atom that perpetually breaks up and forms anew.
>
> (1964: 15)

Luigi Pirandello wrote in his notebook in 1934, 'There is someone who is living my life', adding 'And I know nothing about him' (cited in May 1954: vii).

There is no question that psychoanalysis licenses some kind of postmodern flight into a free-floating world without the necessity for responsibility and choice. Freud foresees no escape from the ego and the decisions it imposes on us. For Lacan the only alternative to the ego and the imaginary would be psychosis or death. Even if always skewed by desire so that it constantly 'neglects', 'misconstrues' and 'ignores' reality (1977a: 22), the 'I' has its place, though one that is temporary and provisional. You do not need *absolute* freedom in order to be held accountable for the decisions human beings have always made.

The 'I' does the best it can though it is always liable to a self-deception we can never be sure of exposing, especially, in Lacan's emphasis, in the very doubt we have 'learned to practise against the traps of self-love' (1977a: 165). The unconscious has an uncanny power to infiltrate your defensive formations so they end up facing another way from the one you thought.

From Aristotle on the advice of the moralists has always been the same: control your passions, don't give in to pleasure. Lacan's book on ethics (1992) makes two simple arguments in reply to this. You cannot do it, and it would not make you happy even if you could.

A comic example would be the case of the American President, Bill Clinton, who told his friend, Dick Morris, 'Ever since the election I've tried to shut my body down, sexually, I mean'. That was his idea but his own desire seems to have had other plans for him and he was forced to add, 'But sometimes I slipped up' (*Sunday Times*, 13 September 1998). A more disturbing example of how 'it' speaks without us even knowing – how someone's look tells a different story from their words – is given by Lacan recalling Freud's account of Ratman. When describing the horrific torture Ratman imagines being applied to the woman he loves, his face reflected 'the horror of a pleasure of which he was unaware' (1977a: 78).

I think it is better for us if we have to accept that desire is endless, that someone else is living our life for us, that in the end (if not before) subjectivity is *impossible*. Utopianism and the ego ideal are pressed in on us from all sides – from television, films, popular music, newspapers, advertising. A hopelessly exaggerated idea of personal happiness and our duty to claim it – for *me*, *now* – has been set up as the obligatory norm for contemporary society. If pursued, this can only lead to despair. As Freud remarks, 'Experience teaches us that the world is no nursery' (1973–86, vol 2: 204).

It is better to be reminded that the subject is impossible. David Cronenberg, who made *Crash* (1996) , said about it in an interview:

> When people talk about movies that could console you, I think this movie could do that. When you're feeling despairing or suicidal, or feel like you're dying, you don't want to see a movie like *Mrs Doubtfire*. A film like *Crash*, *Dead Ringers*, or *Naked Lunch* will console you because they're dealing with this stuff. *Mrs Doubtfire* will kill you.
>
> (*Guardian*, 2 November 1996)

Happy fictions that tell us it will all come right, such as the film of *The Sound of Music* perhaps, are in fact very depressing because they try to conceal unhappiness. It is far better for us to have to come to terms with the idea that desire can never be satisfied and that we will always be incomplete, as films such as *Crash* remind us.

A final story, again about Ratman:

> On the day of her departure [his lover] he knocked his foot against a stone lying in the road, and was *obliged* to put it out of the way by the side of the road, because the idea struck him

that her carriage would be driving along the same road in a few hours' time and might come to grief against this stone. But a few minutes later it occurred to him that this was absurd, and he was *obliged* to go back and replace the stone in its original position in the middle of the road.

(1973–86, vol 9: 70)

The theory of the unconscious means you can never get the stone in the right place.

BIBLIOGRAPHY

Adorno, Theodore (1992) 'On Popular Music', in Antony Easthope and
Kate McGowan (eds), *A Critical and Cultural Theory Reader*,
Buckingham: Open University Press, pp. 211–23.

Althusser, Louis (1977) *Lenin and Philosophy*, trans. Ben Brewster, London:
New Left Books.

Barthes, Roland (1975) *The Pleasure of the Text*, trans. Richard Miller,
Oxford: Blackwell.

Beckett, Samuel (1962) *Malone Dies*, Harmondsworth: Penguin.

Beevor, Antony (1998) *Stalingrad*, London: Viking.

Blake, William (1966) *Complete Writings*, ed. Geoffrey Keynes, London:
Oxford University Press.

Borch-Jacobsen, Mikkel (1990) 'Talking Cure', *Oxford Literary Review* 12:
1–2, 31–55.

Brecht, Bertolt (1964) *Brecht on Theatre*, ed. John Willett, London: Methuen.

Breuilly, John (1982) *Nationalism and the State*, Manchester: Manchester
University Press.

Bryson, Norman (1983) *Vision and Painting: the Logic of the Gaze*, London:
Macmillan.

Cunningham, J.V. (1960) *The Exclusions of a Rhyme*, Denver: Allan
Swallow.

de Rougemont, Denis (1956) *Passion and Society*, rev. edn, trans.
Montgomery Belgion, London: Faber.

Deleuze, Gilles and Guattari, Félix (1988) *A Thousand Plateaus: Capitalism
and Schizophrenia*, trans. Brian Massumi, London: Athlone Press.

Derrida, Jacques (1987) 'Le facteur de la vérité', in *The Post Card*, trans. Alan Bass, Chicago and London: Chicago University Press, pp. 411–96.

Descartes, René (1960) *Discourse on Method*, trans. Laurence J. Lafleur, New York: Liberal Arts.

Easthope, Antony (1989) *Poetry and Phantasy*, Cambridge: Cambridge University Press.

Eliot, T.S. (1966) *Selected Essays*, London: Faber.

Evans, Dylan (1996) 'Historicism and Lacanian Theory', *Radical Philosophy* 79 (September/October): 35–40.

Flaubert, Gustave (1964) *Sentimental Education*, Harmondsworth: Penguin.

Freud, Sigmund (1953–74) *Standard Edition*, 24 vols, London: Hogarth Press and the Institute of Psycho-Analysis.

—— (1973–86) *Pelican Freud Library*, 15 vols, Harmondsworth: Penguin.

Gallup, Jane (1982) *Feminism and Psychoanalysis: the Daughter's Seduction*, London: Macmillan.

Geldof, Bob (1986) *Is That It?* Harmondsworth: Penguin.

Heath, Stephen (1976) '*Anata mo*', *Screen* 17: 4 (Winter): 49–66.

—— (1981) *Questions of Cinema*, London: Macmillan.

Hegel, G.W.F. (1956) *The Philosophy of History*, trans. J. Sibree, New York: Dover.

Hill, Philip (1997) *Lacan for Beginners*, New York: Writers and Readers Publishing.

Hirst, Paul (1979) 'Althusser and the Theory of Ideology', in Paul Q. Hirst, *Law and Ideology*, London: Macmillan, pp. 40–73.

Hirst, Paul and Woolley, Penny (1982) *Social Relations and Human Attributes*, London, Tavistock.

Holland, Norman, N. (1968) *The Dynamics of Literary Response*, New York: Oxford University Press.

—— (1975) *Poems in Persons*, New York: W.W. Norton.

Höss, Rudolf, Broad, P. and Kremer, J.P. (1994) *KL Auschwitz seen by the SS*, The Auschwitz-Birkenau State Museum: Oswiecim.

Isaacs, Susan (1948) 'The Nature and Function of Phantasy', *Internal Journal of Psychoanalysis* 29: 73–97.

Jakobson, Roman (1956) *The Fundamentals of Language*, The Hague: Mouton.

Jameson, Fredric (1977) 'Imaginary and Symbolic in Lacan: Marxism, Psychoanalytic Criticism and the Problem of the Subject', in Shoshana Felman (ed.), *Literature and Psychoanalysis*, *Yale French Studies* 55/56.

—— (1981) *The Political Unconscious: Narrative as a Socially Symbolic Act*, London: Methuen.

Jones, Ernest (1956–58) *Sigmund Freud: Life and Work*, 3 vols, London: Hogarth.

Krafft-Ebing, Richard von (1965) *Psychopathia Sexualis*, trans. Harry E. Wedeck, New York: Putnam.

Kristeva, Julia (1974) *La Révolution du Langage Poétique*, Paris: du Seuil (translated by Margaret Waller (1984) *Revolution in Poetic Language*, New York: Columbia University Press).

—— (1992) 'The System and the Speaking Subject' (1973), reprinted in Antony Easthope and Kate McGowan (eds), *A Critical and Cultural Theory Reader*, Buckingham: Open University Press, pp. 77–80.

—— (1993) *Nations without Nationalism*, trans. Leon S. Roudiez, New York: Columbia University Press.

Lacan, Jacques (1972a) 'Seminar on "The Purloined Letter"', *Yale French Studies* 48: 38–72.

—— (1972b) 'Of Structure as an Inmixing of an Otherness Prerequisite to any Subject Whatever', in Richard Macksey and Eugenio Donato (eds), *The Structuralist Controversy*, Baltimore and London: Johns Hopkins University Press.

—— (1977a) *Ecrits*, trans. Alan Sheridan, London: Tavistock.

—— (1977b) *The Four Fundamental Concepts of Psycho-Analysis*, trans. Alan Sheridan, London: Hogarth.

—— (1977c) 'Desire and Interpretation of Desire in *Hamlet*', trans. James Hulbert, *Yale French Studies* 55/56: 11–52.

—— (1982) *Feminine Sexuality: Jacques Lacan and the 'Ecole Freudienne'*, trans. Jacqueline Rose, London: Macmillan.

—— (1988a) *The Seminar of Jacques Lacan: Book I*, trans. John Forrester, Cambridge: Cambridge University Press.

—— (1977c) 'Desire and Interpretation of Desire in *Hamlet*, trans. James Hulbert, *Yale French Studies* 55/56: 11–52.

—— (1988b) *The Seminar of Jacques Lacan: Book II*, trans. Sylvana Tomaselli, Cambridge: Cambridge University Press.

—— (1992) *The Ethics of Psychoanalysis, 1959–60*, trans. Dennis Porter, London: Tavistock/Routledge.

—— (1993) *The Psychoses, 1955–56*, trans. Russell Grigg, London: Routledge.

Laplanche, Jean, and Pontalis, Jean-Bertrand (1968) 'Fantasy and the Origins of Sexuality', *International Journal of Psychoanalysis* 49 (1): 1–18.

Lapsley, Rob and Westlake, Michael (1993) 'From *Casablanca* to *Pretty Woman*: the Politics of Romance', in Antony Easthope (ed.) *Contemporary Film Theory*, London: Longman, pp. 179–203.

Lazare, Daniel (1998) 'America the Undemocratic', *New Left Review*, November/ December: 3–90.

Lévi-Strauss, Claude (1969) *The Elementary Structures of Kinship*, trans. James Bell and John von Sturmer, Boston, MA: Beacon Press.

Marx, Karl and Engels, Frederick (1950) *Selected Works*, 2 vols, London: Lawrence and Wishart.

May, Frederick (trans.) (1954) *Six Characters in Search of an Author*, London: Heinemann.

Mitchell, Juliet (1975) *Psychoanalysis and Feminism*, Harmondsworth: Penguin.

—— (1982) 'Introduction', *Feminine Sexuality: Jacques Lacan and the 'Ecole Freudienne'*, London: Macmillan, pp. 1–29.

Moi, Toril (1985) *Sexual/Textual Politics*, London: Routledge.

Opie, Iona and Opie, Peter (1959) *The Lore and Language of Schoolchildren*, London: Oxford University Press.

Orwell, George (1984) *Nineteen Eighty-Four*, Harmondsworth: Penguin.

Pound, Ezra (1960) *Gaudier-Brzeska: A Memoir*, Yorkshire: Marvell Press.

Riviere, Joan (1929) 'Womanliness as Masquerade', *International Journal of Psychoanalysis* 10: 303–13.

Roudinesco, Elisabeth (1997) *Jacques Lacan*, Cambridge: Polity.

Saussure, Ferdinand de (1959) *Course in General Linguistics*, trans. Wade Baskin, London: Philosophical Library.

Shelley, Percy Bysshe (1966) 'A Defence of Poetry', in *Selected Poetry and Prose*, ed. Harold Bloom, New York: New American Library.

Sophocles (1965) *Oedipus the King*, trans. David Grene, Chicago: University of Chicago Press.

Stoneman, Patsy (1995) 'Introduction', *Wuthering Heights*, Oxford: Oxford University Press.

Sulloway, Frank (1980) *Freud, Biologist of the Mind*, London: Fontana.

Thompson, Edward (1968) *The Making of the English Working Class*, Harmondsworth: Penguin.

Vygotsky, L.S. (1962) *Thought and Word*, trans. E. Hanfmann and G. Vakar, Cambridge, MA: MIT Press.

Williams, Raymond (1979) *Politics and Letters*, London: New Left Books.

Wordsworth, William (1979) *The Prelude, 1799, 1850, 1850*, Jonathan Wordsworth, M.H. Abrams and Stephen Gill (eds), New York: Norton.

Žižek, Slavoj (1989) *The Sublime Object of Ideology*, London: Verso.

—— (1992) 'In His Bold Gaze My Ruin Is Write Large', in Slavoj Žižek (ed.), *Everything You Always Wanted to Know about Lacan (But Were Afraid to Ask Hitchcock)*, London: Verso, pp. 211–72.

—— (1994) 'Introduction: The Spectre of Ideology', in Slavoj Žižek (ed.), *Mapping Ideology*, London: Verso, pp. 1–33.

INDEX